QUARTERMAINE'S TERMS

Set in the 1960s in a school teaching English to foreigners, Simon Gray's new play follows the varying fortunes of the school and its staff — particularly of St. John Quartermaine, whose naive responses to the emotional crises going on all round him makes him as rich a comic creation as Gray's earlier protagonists, Butley and Simon Hench in *Otherwise Engaged*.

'Mr Gray's selection of details and exchanges is immaculate: he achieves drama and mystery in mundane lives; the comedy is beautifully stated and even personal tragedies are underlined with running gags that ring with truthfulness.'

Ned Chaillet, *The Times*

'One prize at least: Simon Gray's *Quartermaine's Terms* would be major in any year.'

J.C. Trewin, *1981 Drama Awards*

'Best new play.'

Robert Cushman, *1981 Drama Awards*

Quartermaine's Terms won the 1982 Cheltenham Prize for Literature, the first time a play has won this award.

The photograph on the fron... ... from the Queen's Theatre production, ...

The photograph of Simon Gray ... ... cover is reproduced by courtesy of the Sunday Telegr...

Simon Gray

QUARTERMAINE'S TERMS

METHUEN · LONDON AND NEW YORK

A Methuen Paperback

Quartermaine's Terms was first published in 1981 by Eyre
  Methuen Ltd.,
11 New Fetter Lane, London EC4P 4EE
This definitive edition, completely revised and reset, published in
1983 by Methuen London Ltd and Methuen Inc., 733 Third
Avenue, New York 10017
Reprinted 1984
Copyright © 1981, 1983 by Simon Gray
Set in IBM 10pt. Journal by 🅵 Tek-Art, Croydon, Surrey
Printed and bound in Great Britain by Richard Clay (The
Chaucer Press) Ltd., Bungay, Suffolk

ISBN 0 413 52830 8

CAUTION
All rights in this play are strictly reserved and application for
performance etc should be made before rehearsal to Judy Daish
Associates, 122 Wigmore Street, London W1H 9FE. No
performance may be given unless a licence has been obtained.

For BERYL

Quartermaine's Terms was first presented by Michael Codron at the Queen's Theatre, London, on 30 July 1981, with the following cast:

ST. JOHN QUARTERMAINE	Edward Fox
ANITA MANCHIP	Jenny Quayle
MARK SACKLING	Peter Birch
EDDIE LOOMIS	Robin Bailey
DEREK MEADLE	Glyn Grain
HENRY WINDSCAPE	James Grout
MELANIE GARTH	Prunella Scales

Directed by Harold Pinter
Designed by Eileen Diss
Lighting by Leonard Tucker

Quartermaine's Terms was taken on tour by Full Steam Ahead Productions from 24 May to 31 July 1982, with the following cast:

ST. JOHN QUARTERMAINE	Michael Williams
ANITA MANCHIP	Lynne Miller
MARK SACKLING	Michael Bertenshaw
EDDIE LOOMIS	Ernest Clark
DEREK MEADLE	Clive Francis
HENRY WINDSCAPE	Ronald Hines
MELANIE GARTH	Polly James

Directed by Kevin Billington
Designed by Eileen Diss
Lighting by Frederick Curtis

The Set: The staff-room of the Cull-Loomis School of English for foreigners, Cambridge, or rather a section of the staff-room — the last quarter of it. On stage are French windows, a long table, lockers for members of the staff, pegs for coats etc. and a number of armchairs; on the table a telephone, newspapers and magazines. This is the basic set, to which, between scenes and between the two Acts, additions can be made to suggest the varying fortunes of the school. Off stage, left, a suggestion of hard-backed chairs, and off left, a door to the main corridor of the school, where the class-rooms are.

The period: early 1960s.

ACT ONE

Scene One

Monday morning, Spring term. The French windows are open. It is about 9.30. Sunny.

QUARTERMAINE is sitting with his feet up, hands folded on his lap, staring ahead. From off, outside the French windows, in the garden, the sound of foreign voices excited, talking, laughing etc; passing by. As these recede:

ANITA comes through the French windows carrying a briefcase.

QUARTERMAINE. Hello, Anita.

ANITA. 'Morning, St. John.

QUARTERMAINE. But I say, you know, you look different, don't you?

ANITA. Do I? Oh – my hair probably. I've put it up.

QUARTERMAINE. Oh yes. Well, it looks – looks really terrific!

ANITA. Thank you.

QUARTERMAINE. Of course I liked it the other way too, tumbling down your shoulders.

ANITA. It hasn't tumbled down my shoulders for three years St. John.

QUARTERMAINE. Oh. How was it then before you changed it?

ANITA. Back in a pony tail. (*She indicates.*)

QUARTERMAINE. That's it. Yes. Well, I liked it like that, too.

ANITA. Oh by the way, Nigel asked me to apologise again for having to cancel dinner. He was afraid he was a little abrupt on the 'phone.

QUARTERMAINE. Oh Lord, not at all, it was lucky he was, you know how my landlady hates me using the 'phone, but I understood exactly what he was getting at, um — something to do with his new magazine, wasn't it?

ANITA. He still hasn't got enough material for the first issue even. He was up until four, going through all the unsolicited poems and essays and short stories and bits of plays and God knows what. Without much luck, too. He's in despair, poor darling. Anyway, he felt really rotten about messing up *your* evening.

QUARTERMAINE. Oh, do tell him, no need to worry about that. Because as it happened, a few minutes after he 'phoned to cancel, old Henry 'phoned to invite me round there. So that was all right.

ANITA. How smashing! For dinner, you mean?

QUARTERMAINE. Well no, to baby-sit actually.

ANITA. Oh.

QUARTERMAINE. They suddenly remembered there was a film at The Arts, some old um, um German classic that they seem very fond of, about — about a child-murderer as far as I could make out from what Henry said.

ANITA. Still St. John, how boring for you!

QUARTERMAINE. No, no, I enjoyed it enormously, I used to baby-sit for them all the time. It was lovely seeing them again. Children are such . . . And they were as good as gold really, no trouble at all, except that Susan would keep screaming at the little ones. She's working for her 'O' levels you see. The least little bit of noise seems to upset her concentration. But the one they call little Fanny — very charming, very charming. . . . once she'd got used to me again. As for Ben — my word, what a little devil, full of mischief, he told me little Fanny had drowned in the bath and when I ran in, there she was . . . lying face down — hair floating around — and I stood there thinking, you know, (*He laughs.*) Lord, what am I going to say to Henry and Fanny when they get back. Especially after seeing a film like that — but it turned out it was only one of those enormous dolls, you know. (*They both laugh.*)

ANITA. Still St. John, I hope at least you had a bit of an evening with Henry and Fanny when they got back.

QUARTERMAINE. Oh yes. Rather well, except poor old Fanny had a bit of a headache from straining to read the subtitles — a very poor print apparently — and Henry got into a tussle with Susan about going to bed, so I felt you know — that they rather wanted me out of the way —

The sound of the door opening, during the above. Footsteps.

Oh hello Mark, top of the morning to you, have a good weekend?

SACKLING *appears on stage. He is carrying a briefcase, is unshaven, looks ghastly.*

ANITA (*looking at him in concern*). Are you all right?

SACKLING. Yes, yes, fine, fine. (*He drops the briefcase, slumps into chair.*)

ANITA. Are you growing a beard?

SACKLING. What? Oh Christ! (*Feeling his chin.*) I forgot! Haven't been to bed you see. All weekend.

QUARTERMAINE. Ah, been hard at it, eh?

SACKLING. What?

QUARTERMAINE. Hard at it. The old writing.

SACKLING. Oh yes — hard at it.

QUARTERMAINE. Terrific!

ANITA. Oh, I've got a message from Nigel, by the way, he asked me to ask you to hurry up with the extract from your novel, they're desperate to get it into the first issue, he says don't worry about whether it's not quite ready, they can always shove it in as 'Work in Progress' or something.

SACKLING. Right.

ANITA. You look to me as if you've over-done it — are you sure you're all right?

QUARTERMAINE. I say, how's old Camelia?

SACKLING (*barks out a laugh*). Oh fine! just — fine!

QUARTERMAINE. Terrific, and little Tom too?

SACKLING. Tom too, oh yes, Tom too.

QUARTERMAINE. The last time I saw him he was teething, standing there in his high chair dribbling away like anything, while Camelia was sitting on old Mark's lap making faces at him with orange peel in her mouth —

SACKLING *bursts into tears.* ANITA *goes to* SACKLING, *puts her hand on his shoulder.*

QUARTERMAINE. What? Oh — oh Lord!

ANITA. Mark — what is it?

SACKLING. Sorry — sorry — I'll be all right — still digesting.

QUARTERMAINE. Something you had for breakfast, is it?

ANITA *shakes her head at him.*

Mmmm?

ANITA. Do you want to talk about it?

SACKLING. I don't want anyone — anyone else to know — not Thomas or Eddie — don't want them dripping their — their filthy compassion all over me.

ANITA. We're to keep it to ourselves, St. John.

QUARTERMAINE. Oh Lord yes. Of course. (*A pause.*) What though?

SACKLING. She's left me.

QUARTERMAINE. Who?

ANITA. Camelia, of course.

QUARTERMAINE. What! Old Camelia! Oh no!

SACKLING. Taking Tom — taking Tom with her.

QUARTERMAINE. Oh, not little Tom too!

SACKLING. Tom too.

ANITA. Well, did she — say why?

SACKLING (*makes an effort, pulls himself together*). She — (*He takes an envelope out of his pocket.*) I was upstairs in the attic — writing away — as far as I knew she was downstairs where she usually is — in the kitchen or — ironing — with the television on. And Tom in bed, of course. So I wrote on and on — I felt inspired, quite inspired, a passage about — about what I'd felt when I saw Tom coming out of her womb — so shiny and whole and beautiful — a wonderful passage — full of — full of my love for her and him — and when I finished I went downstairs to her — to read it to her — as I always do when it's something I'm burning with — and this was on the pillow. (*He opens the letter.*) 'I'm sorry darling, but it seems after all that I wasn't cut out to be a writer's wife. I can't stand the strain of it, the lonely evenings, your remoteness, and most of all the feeling that your novel means more to you than Tom and I do. Perhaps that's what being an artist is. Not caring about those who love you. I'm going back to mother's, I'll take the car' — yes, taken the car — she'd take that all right, wouldn't she! — 'until you've passed your driving test' and begin proceedings as soon as I've got a lawyer. Take care, my love, look after yourself, I wish you such success and I know that one day I'll be proud to have been your first wife, just as Tom will be proud to be your father.'

There is a pause.

QUARTERMAINE. Um, son, surely.

SACKLING. What?

QUARTERMAINE. Um, Tom's your son. Not your father. You read out that he was your father. Not your son.

SACKLING. Oh, if only I'd been able to read her that passage — she would have understood my feelings, she'd have known — but what do I do, I can't give up my novel now, not when I'm so close to finishing — my fourth draft — my penultimate draft — I *know* it's the penultimate — then one final one — and — and — so what do I do —

LOOMIS *enters through the French windows. He walks awkwardly, has thick glasses, is carrying a file.*

LOOMIS. Good morning, good morning, Anita my dear, Mark,
St. John. I trust you all had a good weekend?

QUARTERMAINE.
ANITA.   } Yes, thank you Eddie.
SACKLING.

LOOMIS. I'm just on my way through to do my little welcome
speech to the new students, with a small dilation this time on
the problems of our Cambridge landladies, we've just heard
that our faithful Mrs Cornley is refusing to take any of our
students except what she calls traditional foreigners, all over
some dreadful misunderstanding she's had with those three
really delightful Turks we sent her, over the proper function
of the bathroom — such a nuisance, Thomas has been on the
'phone to her for hours — but still, I suppose the problems
of a flourishing school — nine Japanese have turned up, by
the way, instead of the anticipated six, and as it was three last
time we can hope for a round dozen next — Mark, is it these
fast-fading old eyes of mine, or did you forget to shave this
morning, and yesterday morning, even?

SACKLING. No, no — I'm thinking of growing a beard, Eddie.

LOOMIS. Alas! And what saith the fair Camelia to that?

SACKLING (*mutters*). I don't think she'll mind, Eddie.

LOOMIS. Good, good — Anita, my dear, may I pay you a
compliment?

ANITA. Yes please, Eddie.

LOOMIS. I like your hair even more *that* way.

ANITA. Well, thank you Eddie, actually I had it cut for a dinner
party we had last night — so I suppose I'm stuck with it for a
bit — it was a sort of editorial dinner, you see — (*Realising.*)

LOOMIS. Ah! And the magazine's progressing well, or so we
gathered from Nigel. We bumped into him on the Backs, on
Saturday afternoon, did he tell you?

ANITA. No. No he didn't.

LOOMIS. He was having a conference with one of his co-editors,
I suppose it was.

ANITA. Oh. Jeffrey Pine.

LOOMIS. No no, I don't think Jeffrey Pine, my dear, but co-editress I should have said, shouldn't I, one can't be too precise these days.

ANITA. Oh. Was she — blonde and — rather pretty?

LOOMIS. Oh, very pretty — at least Thomas was much smitten, you know what an eye he's got.

ANITA. Ah, then that would be Amanda Southgate, yes, I expect he was trying to persuade her to take on all the dog-bodying — you know, hounding contributors, keeping the printers at bay — she's terrifically efficient. She's an old friend of mine. We were at school together. (*Little pause.*) She's smashing, actually.

LOOMIS. Good good — now St. John, what was it Thomas asked me to tell you — or was it Henry and Melanie I'm to tell what to? Oh yes, this postcard of course, from one of your old students. (*He hands him a post-card from the file.*) We couldn't resist having a look, post-cards being somehow in the public domain, one always thinks. At least when they're other people's. (*He laughs.*) Do read it out to Mark and Anita, don't be modest St. John.

QUARTERMAINE. Um, I must writing to thanking you for all excellent times in your most glorified classes, your true Ferdinand Muller. Lord! (*He laughs.*)

LOOMIS. And which one was he, can you recall?

QUARTERMAINE. Oh. Well, you know a — a German —

LOOMIS. Post-marked Zurich, I believe, so more likely a Swiss.

QUARTERMAINE. Oh yes, that's right, a Swiss, a — a well, rather large, Eddie, and with a round face — in his forties or so, with his hair cut en brosse.

LOOMIS. — and wearing lederhosen, perhaps, and good at yodelling, no no, St. John, I don't think I quite believe in your rather caricature Swiss, I suspect you must have made rather more of an impression on Herr Ferdinand Muller than he managed to make on you, still, I suppose that's better than the other way round, and his sentiments are certainly quite a tribute — would that his English were, too eh? But do try to remember them St. John, match names to faces. (*He laughs.*) And on that subject, you haven't forgotten Mr Middleton begins this morning, have you?

QUARTERMAINE. Who, Eddie?

LOOMIS. Middleton. Dennis Middleton, St. John. Our new part timer. Thomas told you all about him at the last staff meeting. He should be here any minute — so whilst I'm making the students welcome, perhaps you'd do the same for him, and tell him that either Thomas or I will be along before the bell. Mark?

SACKLING. Mmm?

LOOMIS. Middleton, Mark.

SACKLING (*blankly*). Yes. Yes. Right Eddie.

LOOMIS. Good good. See you all at the bell then — (*He walks off, stage left. Sound of him stopping. Slight pause.*) Oh Mark, there is one other thing — If I could just have a quick private word — May I put in my personal plea against the beard, I do think they make even the handsomest chaps red-eyed and snivelly looking, I don't want to end up begging Camelia to be Delilah to your Samson, eh, and think of poor little Tom too, having to endure Daddy's whiskers against his chubby young cheeks at cuddle-time —

SACKLING *rushes past him, out of the door.*

But — but — what did I say? It was only about about the beard, I couldn't have been more playful.

QUARTERMAINE. Oh, it's not your fault, Eddie, is it Anita, the poor chap's had a — a horrible weekend — you see —

ANITA (*warningly, cutting in*). Yes, up all night, working at his novel. I'll go and see if he's all right. (*She goes off, left.*)

LOOMIS. I see. Well that's all very well, after all nobody could respect Mark's literary ambitions more than Thomas and myself, but we really can't have him running about in this sort of state, what on earth would the students make of it if he were to gallop emotionally off in the middle of a dictation —

MEADLE appears at the French windows.

MEADLE. Um, is this the staff room, please?

He is hot and flustered, wearing bicycle clips, carrying a briefcase.

LOOMIS. Yes, what do you want?

MEADLE. I'm the new member of staff.

LOOMIS. Oh, of course, it's Mr Middleton, isn't it?

MEADLE. Well, yes — well, Meadle, actually, Derek Meadle.

LOOMIS. Yes, yes, Derek Meadle, well, I'm Eddie Loomis, the Principal. One of two Principals, as you know, as you've met Mr Cull of course, and this is St. John Quartermaine who's been with us since our school started, and you've come down to join us from Huddersfield, isn't it.

MEADLE. Yes sir, well Hull actually.

LOOMIS. Hull, good good — and when did you arrive?

MEADLE. Yesterday afternoon.

LOOMIS. And found yourself a room?

MEADLE. Yes, yes thank you, sir.

LOOMIS. Good good, and found yourself a bicycle too, I see.

MEADLE (*who throughout all this has been standing rather awkwardly keeping face on to* LOOMIS). Yes, sir. My landlady — I happened to ask her where could be a good place to buy a second-hand one, not being familiar with the shops, and she happened to mention that her son had left one behind in the basement and I could have it for two pounds, but unfortunately —

LOOMIS (*interrupting*). Good good, most enterprising — at least of your landlady. (*He laughs.*) But Mr Meadle I've got to have a little talk with the students, and Mr Cull is still looking after enrolment, but one of us will be back at the bell to introduce you to your first class — intermediary comprehension isn't it —

MEADLE. Dictation sir.

LOOMIS. Quite. So I'll leave you in St. John's capable hands —

MEADLE. Yes sir. Thank you.

LOOMIS. Oh, one thing, though, Mr Meadle — sir us no sirs, we're very informal here — I'm Eddie, Mr Cull is Thomas and you're Dennis.

MEADLE. Oh, well thank you very much —

LOOMIS *goes off left.*

Derek actually —

QUARTERMAINE. Well, I must say — jolly glad to have you with us — I think you'll enjoy it here — the staff is — well, they're terrific — and the students are — well, they've very interesting, coming as they do from all quarters of the globe, so to speak — but look here, why don't you sit down and make yourself at home.

MEADLE. Yes, thanks, but — well, you see the trouble is I've had a bit of an accident.

QUARTERMAINE. Oh really? Oh Lord.

MEADLE. Yes, well — you'd better see for yourself.

He turns. His trousers are rent at the seat.

How bad is it actually?

QUARTERMAINE. Well — they're a bit of a write off, I'm afraid. How did it happen?

MEADLE. Some bloody Japanese! I rode into a little pack of them coming up the school drive. They were laughing and chattering so much among themselves they didn't hear my bell until I was almost on top of them, and then a big, bald one stepped right out in front of me and of course I lost control on the gravel and skidded.

QUARTERMAINE. Oh dear.

MEADLE. And as there was the minutest bit of spring sticking out of the seat — I suppose it must have worked its way into my trousers on the way here — the worm in the apple, eh?

But anyway — what do you think I should do about it?

QUARTERMAINE. Well you know, old chap, I think the best thing would be to go back and change.

MEADLE. Ah yes, but into what is the question.

QUARTERMAINE. Well — into another pair of trousers, I — I suppose.

MEADLE. Yes, but you see, I haven't got another pair is the problem. An elderly gentleman on the train yesterday spilt hot chocolate out of his thermos right over the pair I happened to have on, so the first thing I did when I got in — irony of ironies — was to take them to the cleaners. And my trunk, which I'd sent on from Hull and which contained my suit and my other two pairs, hasn't arrived yet. So there it is. What do I do? Any suggestions? I mean if I pull them really high — like this — and leave my clips on — well how do I look?

QUARTERMAINE. Well, well, jolly formidable, actually.

MEADLE (*takes a few more steps*). No, no, I can't go round like this! I'm meant to be teaching — people will think I'm sort of — some sort of — my first day of my new job — oh, this is the sheerest, the sheerest — !

WINDSCAPE (*enters through the French windows. He is carrying a brief-case, wears bicycle clips, smokes a pipe. Seeing MEADLE*). Ah —

QUARTERMAINE. Hello Henry — um, come and meet our new chap —

WINDSCAPE. Oh yes, of course. Merton, isn't it?

QUARTERMAINE. Middleton, actually.

MEADLE. Meadle, as a matter of fact.

QUARTERMAINE. Meadle. That's right. So sorry. Dennis Meadle.

WINDSCAPE (*comes over*). Well, whatever yours happens to be — mine's Windscape. Henry Windscape. How do you do.

MEADLE. How do you do.

WINDSCAPE. Very glad to have you with us.

MEADLE. Thank you.

QUARTERMAINE. Henry's our academic tutor — syllabus and all that.

MEADLE. Oh.

WINDSCAPE. Oh, St. John, I didn't thank you properly last night for baby-sitting. It was most kind.

QUARTERMAINE. Oh, not at all — I enjoyed it. I say, how were they in the end — Susan, little Fanny and old Ben?

WINDSCAPE. Oh fine thank you, St. John, fine. I didn't get Susan to bed until midnight of course. (*To* MEADLE:) She's studying for her 'O' levels — a couple of years in advance.

QUARTERMAINE. And what about Fanny's headache?

WINDSCAPE. Oh fine thank you, fine. Though she did have rather a bad moment actually, when she went to have her bath and thought little Fanny was lying in it — drowned.

QUARTERMAINE. Oh yes — that blessed doll.

WINDSCAPE. Yes, Ben told me you'd put it there. St. John was good enough to come over and sit with our three last night — we went to see *M* you know — such a fine film — so delicate and human in its treatment of a — a sexual freak, and Peter Lorre — unfortunately the print was a trifle worn — but still — memorable — memorable — but isn't it interesting — on another subject — this English thing about names, how we forget them the second we hear them. Just now, for instance, when St. John was introducing you. Unlike Americans for instance. (*He puffs and pulls on his pipe throughout this speech.* MEADLE *nods and chuckles tensely.*) I suppose because we — the English that is — are so busy looking at the person the name represents — or *not* looking, being English (*He laughs.*) that we don't take in the name itself — whereas the Americans, you see, make a point of beginning with the name — when one's introduced they repeat it endlessly. 'This is Dennis Meadle. Dennis Meadle, why hello Dennis, and how long have you been in this country Dennis, this is Dennis Meadle dear, Dennis was just telling me how much he liked our fair city, weren't you Dennis . . . ' (*All this is an execrable imitation of an American accent.*) And — and so forth.

MEADLE (*tacit*). Derek actually.

WINDSCAPE. And in no time at all they've learnt what you're called by even if not who you are (*He laughs.*) while we, the English, being more empirical, don't learn your name until you yourself have taken on a complicated reality — you and your name grow, so to speak, in associated stages in our memories, until what you are as Dennis Meadle and the sounds Dennis Meadle are inseparable which is actually — when you think about it, a radical division in ways of perceiving that goes back to the Middle Ages in the Nominalists — the name callers — calling the name preceeding the object, so to speak, and the realists —

During this, MELANIE *has entered through the French windows. She puts her briefcase on the table.*

— who believed the object preceeded the name — but one could go on and on; and, there's Melanie, come and meet (*A pause.*) our new chap —

MELANIE. You're in top form for a Monday morning Henry, how do you do, I'm Melanie Garth.

MEADLE. Meadle. Derek Meadle.

MELANIE. And you've come to reinforce us, well we certainly could do with you, Thomas was just telling me about the enrolment chaos, you'll be getting a lot of overspill from my groups, I can tell you.

WINDSCAPE. Melanie's our Elementary Conversation specialist, by the way.

MELANIE. Oh, I don't know about specialist, Henry, Henry's our only real specialist here, he specialises in — well, everything, doesn't he, St. John, from pronounciation to British Life and Institutions, but what I enjoyed most about the sight of you two philosophising away here was that you both still had your bicycle clips on — as if you'd met on a street corner —

WINDSCAPE (*laughing*). Good heavens, so they are. Thank you for reminding me, my dear, whenever I forget to take them off I spend hours after school hunting for them — (*He bends, to take them off.*)

MEADLE *grinning and distraught, makes a gesture towards taking his off.*

QUARTERMAINE (*taking this in*). I say — I say, Melanie, how's — um, how's mother?

MELANIE. Top form, thanks, St. John, her left leg's still giving her bother, and the stairs are a dreadful strain, you know, because of this sudden vertigo, but yesterday she managed to hobble down to the corner-shop all by herself, and was halfway back by the time I got there to pick her up.

QUARTERMAINE. Oh, that's terrific! Melanie's mother's just recovering from a thingemebob.

MELANIE. Stroke, if you please, St. John. She insists on the proper term, she hates euphemisms.

WINDSCAPE. Not surprisingly, as Melanie's mother was Cambridge's first lady of philology — I had the honour of being supervised by her in my second year as an undergraduate. A remarkable woman who seems to be coming to terms with her little upset in a characteristically — characteristically indomitable — fashion.

MEADLE. I have an aunt who had a stroke a year ago. She was the active sort too.

MELANIE. And how is *she* coping?

MEADLE. Well, she was doing splendidly until she had the next. Now she's pretty well out of it altogether, my uncle has to do virtually everything for her. But then that's one of the usual patterns, they said at the hospital. First a mild stroke, followed by a worse stroke, and then, if that doesn't do the job — (*He gestures.*)

MELANIE. Yes, well, Mr Meadle, I'm sorry for your aunt — and for your uncle — but sufficient unto the day, sufficient unto the day. (*She picks up her briefcase and goes to a locker.*)

WINDSCAPE. Of course that's only *one* of the possible patterns —

there are many cases of complete — or — or more than merely partial recovery — Dennis, if I might — might just — Melanie puts on a remarkably brave front, but don't be led astray, she's an intensely feeling person who knows very well the likely outcome of her mother's — her mother's - she's deeply attached to her, as you probably gathered.

I hope you don't mind my er —

MEADLE. No, no. Thank you. Thank you.

WINDSCAPE. Good man! (*He puts his hand on MEADLE's shoulder.*) Well, I'd better unpack my own — (*He goes over to a locker, looking towards MELANIE, who is still standing still by hers.*)

MELANIE (*whispered*). Well naught out of ten for tact, I thought!

WINDSCAPE (*whispered*). Yes well, it is his first day, Melanie my dear — he didn't really understand.

MEADLE (*crossing to QUARTERMAINE*). I don't think I can stand much more of this. I hardly know what I'm saying. Look, what I need is some safety pins and a few minutes in the toilet.

QUARTERMAINE. Yes, of course, you come along with me.

LOOMIS (*comes through the French windows*). Good morning, Melanie, my dear. Good morning Henry — good weekend, I trust?

MELANIE.
WINDSCAPE. } Yes thanks, Eddie.

QUARTERMAINE (*to MEADLE*). Better hang on a tick.

LOOMIS. All well with mother, I trust?

MELANIE. Yes thanks Eddie. Top form.

LOOMIS. Good, good — and Fanny and the children?

WINDSCAPE. Yes, thanks Eddie — all splendid.

LOOMIS. Good good —

As ANITA and SACKLING enter from right.

Ah, and here you are, you two, and quite composed again Mark, I trust —

ANITA. Well Eddie, actually I'm not sure that Mark's quite up to it.

SACKLING *feebly gestures silence to* ANITA.

LOOMIS. And Mr Meadle, I don't know which of you had the chance to meet him yet, but those who haven't can make their separate introductions, in the meanwhile I'll say a welcome on all our behalves, we're delighted to have you with us — I see you've still got your clips on, by the way.

MEADLE. Oh yes.

LOOMIS. Perhaps you'd better remove them or you'll create the impression that you're just pedalling through — (*He laughs.*)

MEADLE *bends, to take them off.*

Good — now as we're all here and there are a few minutes before the bell, I'd like to say a few words, if I may. So, gather ye round — gather ye round. (*They all do so.*) As you've no doubt realised, we have an exceptionally high enrolment for the month, the highest in the school's career, as a matter of fact. (*Little murmurs.*)

QUARTERMAINE. I say, terrific!

LOOMIS. Yes, very gratifying. You all know how hard Thomas has worked for this. Though he'd loathe to hear me say it. But what he wouldn't mind hearing me say is that in his turn he knows how hard you've worked. I think we all have a right to be proud of our growing reputation as one of the best schools of English — not one of the biggest but one of the best — in Cambridge. Which, when it comes down to it, means in the country.

ALL. Murmur.

MELANIE (*murmurs*). Solemn thought.

LOOMIS. Well and good. Well and good. But success will bring — has already begun to bring — its own problems. (*He gestures to* MEADLE.) As Mr Meadle's presence here testifies. But even with Mr Meadle — or Dennis, as I've already told him I intend to call him — with Dennis to help us, there is going to be a considerable strain on our resources. Perhaps a few too many students to a classroom, more work to take home and correct, more difficulties in developing personal contact — that so crucial personal contact —

QUARTERMAINE. Absolutely crucial.

LOOMIS. Many of whom are only here for a short time — well, as I say, you've already become familiar with the problems, the problems, as Thomas remarked 'midst the chaos this morning, of a flourishing school —

SACKLING *faints.*

ANITA. Oh my God!

ANITA *cries out.*
WINDSCAPE *gets to him.*

WINDSCAPE. The thing is to — (*He puts his hand on* SACKLING's *heart.*) His heart — I can't feel his heart —

A pause.

QUARTERMAINE (*also looking down*). Oh Lord!

The bell rings.

Lights.

Scene Two

QUARTERMAINE. Oh Lord! Hello Eddie.

LOOMIS. You're in sprightly mood, St. John.

QUARTERMAINE. Friday evening you know — and I'm off to the theatre tonight with old Mark and Anita.

LOOMIS. And what are you going to see?

QUARTERMAINE. Oh that — that Strinberg, I think it is. At The Arts.

LOOMIS. I believe it's an Ibsen, Hedda Gabler — I believe.

QUARTERMAINE. Oh, is it really?

LOOMIS. But tell me, the bell's gone then, has it, I didn't hear it — but then these old ears of mine —

QUARTERMAINE. Ah yes, well I let them out a little early, you see Eddie.

LOOMIS. Why?

QUARTERMAINE. Well, it was my turn to give the advance British Life and Institutions Lecture, and I chose Oxford Colleges — to give them the other point of view, for once — illustrated with slides, but I'd only just got going, and blow me tight — the old projector broke.

LOOMIS. Broke? But we've only just bought it. It's the newest model.

QUARTERMAINE. Yes, I think that's part of the problem, all those extra bits to master — anyway, one of the colleges went in upside down and wouldn't come out so I had to — to abandon technology and do it all off my own bat — you know, reminiscences of my time at the House and — and anedotes — and — you know — that sort of thing. The personal touch. But of course I ran out of steam a little, towards the end, I'm afraid.

LOOMIS. And how many turned up?

QUARTERMAINE. Oh well — about a handful.

LOOMIS. A handful!

QUARTERMAINE. A good handful.

LOOMIS. But there are meant to be twenty-three in the group that that special lecture's designed for.

QUARTERMAINE. Yes, well I think you know — it's being Friday and — and the sun shining and the Backs so lovely and the Cam jam-packed with punts and — but the ones who did come were jolly interested — especially that little Italian girl — you know um — um — almost midget sized, the one with the wart —

LOOMIS. If you mean Angelina, she happens to be Greek. Her father's an exceptionally distinguished army officer. Thomas will be very disappointed to hear about all this, St. John, he devised that lecture series himself, you know, it's quite an innovation, and if you can't keep attendances up — and you know very well how important it is to keep classes going until at least the bell — ah, hello my dear, you've finished a trifle on the early side too, then?

ANITA. Oh, isn't it past five?

LOOMIS. Well, the bell hasn't gone yet, even in your part of the corridor — intermediary dictation, wasn't it, and how was your attendance?

ANITA. Oh, nearly a full complement, Eddie, they're a very keen lot, mostly Germans, in fact that's why I thought the bell had gone, one of them said he'd heard it.

LOOMIS. Which one?

ANITA. I think it was Kurt.

LOOMIS. I see.

ANITA *makes to go to her locker.*

LOOMIS. My dear, have I told you what I think about your sandals?

ANITA. No, Eddie.

QUARTERMAINE. I think they're smashing.

LOOMIS. Well, when I first saw you in them I wondered if they were quite *comme il fault,* Thomas and I had quite a thing about them — but I've been quite won around, I've come to the view that they're most fetching. Or that your feet are. Or both. (*He laughs.*)

ANITA. Thank you, Eddie.

LOOMIS. And Nigel's still in London, is he, with his co-editress?

ANITA. Yes, he comes back on Saturday or Sunday.

LOOMIS. Quite a coincidence Thomas seeing them on the train like that, he's scarcely been out of his office this many a month, as you know — and it's all working out all right, is it?

ANITA. Yes, Amanda's been absolutely wonderful, quite a surprise really, because when I first met her at a party a few months ago, I thought she was — well, absolutely charming, of course, but rather — rather feckless, if anything. But it turns out she's got a really good tough brain. Her boyfriend's being a great help too. He's invaluable.

LOOMIS. But you met her at a party. How odd, I had an idea you went to school with her?

ANITA (*slight hesitation*). No no — with her sister, Seraphina.

LOOMIS. Ah yes — but I was really asking about the magazine itself, how that was coming?

ANITA. Oh, they've finally settled on a title. It's going to be called *Reports.*

QUARTERMAINE. Terrific!

LOOMIS. *Reports.*

The bell rings.

Reports, mmm, well, tell Nigel when he gets back that Thomas has decided to take out *two* subscriptions, one for ourselves and one for the student common room, so we'll be showing a great personal interest —

ANITA. Oh thank you, Eddie, Nigel will be so pleased —

From the garden, the sound of WINDSCAPE, *off.*

WINDSCAPE (*off*). I can't stay too long, I'm afraid, just to start you off and explain the rules — but first let's get the mallets and balls —

The voices recede.

LOOMIS (*going to the window*). Ah, the croquet's under way again, good, good, — and who's playing — ah, Piccolo and Jean-Pierre, Gisela — Teresa — Okona — Liv and Gerta — you know, I always feel that if ever our little school had to justify itself, we could do it by showing the world the spectacle of an Italian, a Frenchman, a German, a Japanese, a Swedish girl and a Belgian girl, all gathered together on an English lawn, under an English sky to play a game of croquet —

ANITA *through this has gone to her locker.*

QUARTERMAINE. Absolutely, Eddie, absolutely — croquet —

I must try my hand again — haven't for years — not since my
aunt's when I was a child — she had such a lawn, you know, and
I remember, oh Lord, (*Shaking his head, laughing.*) Oh Lord,
I say, I forgot, Thomas told me to tell you he was looking
for you.

LOOMIS. Thomas? When?

QUARTERMAINE. Oh, just at the end of my lecture — he
popped his head in.

LOOMIS. Really, St. John, I wish you'd mentioned it straight
away, it would have to be something urgent for Thomas to
interrupt a class — was he going back to the office?

SACKLING *enters, during this. Carrying books, etc. He sports
a moustache.*

QUARTERMAINE. He didn't say, Eddie.

LOOMIS. Mark, have you happened to glimpse Thomas —

SACKLING. Yes. I think he and Melanie were going up to your
flat —

LOOMIS. Oh. Well, if he should come down here looking for me,
tell him I've gone upstairs to the flat — and that I'll stay there
so that we don't do one of our famous boxes and coxes —
(*He goes out left.*)

SACKLING. Right Eddie. (*Going to his locker.*)

ANITA, *during the above, has finished packing, is leaving.
There is an air of desperate rush about her.*

QUARTERMAINE. Wasn't he in a dodgy mood — but I say, where
shall we meet, Anita, shall Mark and I come and pick you
up at your place, or shall we go to Mark's place, or the foyer,
or — or we could go to The Eagle — or you two could come
to my place —

ANITA. Oh, I'm sorry, St. John, I completely forgot — you see
I'm going to London. It suddenly occurred to me that as Nigel
can't get back until tomorrow or Sunday, why not pop down
and spend the weekend with him.

QUARTERMAINE. What a good idea. Much more fun than some

old Ibsen thing.

SACKLING. Does he know you're coming?

ANITA. No, it's a surprise.

SACKLING. Shouldn't you 'phone him first? I mean he may be going out or — you know.

ANITA. I haven't got time. Look, I've got to dash if I'm going to make the five-thirty — damn Eddie! (*Rushing off.*)

SACKLING. Oh Christ! Poor old Nigel.

QUARTERMAINE. Mmmm?

SACKLING. Well, surely you know?

QUARTERMAINE. What?

SACKLING. About Nigel and Amanda Southgate. They're having a passionate affair. He only started the magazine because of her — she's got literary ambitions.

QUARTERMAINE. Oh — oh, Lord, poor old Anita! But they always seemed so happy —

SACKLING. You know, St. John, you have an amazing ability not to let the world impinge on you. Anita's the unhappiest woman I know, at the moment. And has been, ever since she met Nigel. Amanda's his fifth affair in the last two years, even if the most serious. But Anita covers up for him, pretends it isn't happening, or tries to protect a reputation he hasn't got and probably doesn't want anyway, he's made her have three abortions although she's desperate for children — haven't you had the slightest inkling of any of that?

QUARTERMAINE. No.

SACKLING. But what I don't understand is why she's suddenly gone down to confront him. She's only survived so far by not daring to have anything out with him — she's never once mentioned even the most blatant of his infidelities, actually that's one of the things about her that drives him mad. Anyway, there's nothing we can do about it, is there? I haven't even got his number, so I can't warn him.

QUARTERMAINE. Don't you like Anita?

SACKLING. Of course I do. Far more than I like Nigel, as a matter of fact.

QUARTERMAINE. Oh. Oh well it all seems — all seems — I mean these things between people — people one cares for — it's hard to bear them — but, but I say, what about this evening then, how would you like to play it? Eagle or — shall we meet at the theatre?

SACKLING. As a matter of fact, St. John, I'm going to have to bow out of the theatre, too.

QUARTERMAINE. Oh. Oh well —

SACKLING. You see, last night I went back to it again. My novel. The first time since Camelia left. And there was the old flame aflickering as strongly as ever. So I've got to get back to it this evening. Look, you haven't actually bought the tickets, have you?

QUARTERMAINE (*makes to say yes, changes his mind*). No, no, never any need to at the Arts, so don't worry about that but — but it's terrific that you've starting writing again, that's far more important than going to see some — some old Ibsen thing.

SACKLING. Thanks. And St. John, thanks also for your companionship these last weeks. It must have been bloody boring for you, having me grind on and on in my misery.

QUARTERMAINE. Lord no, I've enjoyed it enormously. Not your misery I don't mean but your (*He laughs.*) — your — but I say, have you heard from Camelia?

SACKLING. Yes, this morning. She's allowing me a few hours tomorrow afternoon. With my son.

QUARTERMAINE. But that's wonderful, Mark. Look, when will you be back?

SACKLING. Tomorrow evening, I suppose.

QUARTERMAINE. Well, perhaps we could have lunch on Sunday or dinner or meet for a drink — and you could tell me how things went with little Tom — I'd really love to know.

During this, the sound of the door opening, closing, followed by a yelp.

MEADLE (*off*). Blast!

QUARTERMAINE. You all right, old man?

MEADLE (*he is wearing a suit, has a bump on his forehead, covered by a piece of sticking plaster*). Yes, yes — (*Rubbing his hand.*) It's that door-knob, a bit too close to the door-jamb — at least for my taste — (*He laughs.*) I'm always scraping my knuckles on it — hello, Mark, haven't seen you around for a bit, I suppose because you're usually gone before I finish.

SACKLING. Don't worry, I do my time. Right to the bell.

MEADLE. Oh, I didn't mean any reflection — (*He laughs.*) Good God, I only meant that I always seem to get caught by students who want to practise their English after hours too — of course it doesn't help to be carrying a conversation piece around on your forehead — What 'appen 'ead, Mr Mittle, whasa matter weet de het, Meester Meetle, Mister Mittle vat goes mit der hed b- (*Laughing.*) up the corridor, down, in the classroom, in the garden — by the time I'd gone through all the details, with pantomime, landlady calling to the telephone, toe stubbing in cracked linoleum, body pitching down the stairs and bonce cracking down on tile I'd have settled for serious internal injuries instead.

SACKLING (*smiles*). Goodnight. (*He goes out through the French windows.*)

QUARTERMAINE (*who has been laughing with* MEADLE). Oh, night old man, but oh, just a minute, we haven't fixed our meeting — (*He goes to the French windows, stares out.*)

MEADLE (*who has registered* SACKLING's *manner*). He's a hard chap to get to know, isn't he?

QUARTERMAINE. Who? Old Mark? Lord no — oh, well perhaps to begin with but once you do know him you can't imagine a — a better friend.

MEADLE. Oh. Well, I'll keep working on it then. (*Going to his locker.*)

QUARTERMAINE. I say, I've managed to get hold of some tickets for the theatre tonight. They're doing an Ibsen! Would you like to come?

MEADLE. To tell you the truth, Ibsen's not quite my cup of tea, thanks, but anyway as a matter of fact Oko-Ri's taking me out to dinner tonight with the rest of the boys.

QUARTERMAINE. Oko — what?

MEADLE. Ri. Oko-Ri. My Japanese chum.

QUARTERMAINE. Oh, old baldy, you mean? Taking you out to dinner — well, that's — that's — I didn't know you'd hit it off so well with them, after your trouser —

MEADLE. Well, I never thought they'd made me skid deliberately — and we've had lots of good laughs about it since — now that I'm on their wave-length — Oko-Ri's got a splendid sense of humour. Loves a drink too, I gather, from some of their jokes.

QUARTERMAINE. Oh, well, you'll have a good evening then —

MEADLE. It's really just to say thank you for all the extra hours I've put in with them. They left it to me to decide where we'd go, and I've chosen that French place that's just opened opposite Trinity, Eddie and Thomas were saying it's very good.

QUARTERMAINE. So I hear.

MEADLE. Anyway, I'd better get back. I'd ask you to come along too, but it's not really my invitation —

QUARTERMAINE. No, no — I quite understand.

The sound of the door opening and closing, feet.

MEADLE. Oh. Here. Let me give you a hand with those, Melanie —

MELANIE (*off*). No, it's quite all right, I've got them —

MEADLE (*off*). Well, let me just take this one —

MELANIE. No, no, really — there's no need —

The sound of books dropping on the floor.

MEADLE (*off*). Oh, sorry, Melanie —

MELANIE (*irritably*). Oh — really! I had them perfectly well — and Thomas has just lent me that one with great warnings to be careful, it's a rare edition —

MEADLE *coming on stage, carrying a distinguished volume.*

(*Coming on stage, carrying a briefcase, exercise books and further books.*) If you could just put it on the table — Have either of you seen Eddie, Thomas has been looking for him.

QUARTERMAINE. Now what did Eddie say — oh yes, that he was going to wait for Thomas in the — in the office, it must have been.

MELANIE. Oh, good, well that's where Thomas has gone — so you're the last two then, are you?

QUARTERMAINE. Yes, well apart from old Henry, that is, he's playing croquet —

MELANIE. Is he, jolly good! (*She goes to her locker.*)

MEADLE (*who has been looking through the book*). No, no damage done, Melanie. (*He looks at his watch.*) So Thomas is in the office, is he?

MELANIE. Yes, why, what do you want him for?

MEADLE. Oh — well — well actually he said something about seeing if he could get me some extra pronunciation classes — as I'm part-time, I need all the hours I can get, you see. (*He laughs.*)

MELANIE. I wouldn't go disturbing him now, if I were you, he's had a particularly fraught day. He's got a dreadful headache. The only person he'll want to see is Eddie.

MEADLE. Oh. Well, in that case, goodnight, Melanie.

MELANIE. Goodnight — oh, that reminds me, I'd be very grateful if you'd stop putting your bicycle against the wall where I park my car — there's not enough room for both.

MEADLE. Oh, sorry about that — right Melanie — well, see you Monday then.

QUARTERMAINE. See you Monday, old man. (*As MEADLE goes out through the French windows.*)

MELANIE. I really think I'd get on much better with Mr Meadle if he didn't try so hard to get on with me.

MEADLE (*meanwhile, off*). 'Night Henry, see you Monday.

WINDSCAPE (*off*). Oh. 'Night Derek. Have a good weekend.

MEADLE (*off*). Thanks, Henry — same to you.

MELANIE. Still, apparently he works very hard at his teaching, from all accounts. Thomas and Eddie are both rather thrilled with him. And really I had no right to stop him from seeing Thomas — not my business at all. But Thomas really is in a terrible state. He's spent the whole afternoon on the telephone because of that wretched Jap — the big, bald one, you know — apparently he got drunk and ran amok in that new French restaurant last night, and the owners are demanding damages and threatening to call the police, if he shows up again, and then one of the other Japanese turned up at lunch-time to book a table for tonight — Goodness knows what's going to happen if the bald one appears too. Well, St. John, and what are your plans for the weekend, something on the boil, I'll bet!

QUARTERMAINE. Oh, well I thought I might take in a show tonight — that Ibsen thing at the Arts —

MELANIE. Isn't it *The Cherry Orchard*?

QUARTERMAINE. Oh, is it? Well — something terrific like that. And then a bit of supper, I suppose. I might try that French place in fact. Might be rather — rather amusing. (*He laughs.*)

MELANIE. It must be jolly nice being a bachelor and having the weekend before you. Especially in Cambridge.

QUARTERMAINE. Yes, terrific fun.

MELANIE. Well, I'd better get on with this. I don't think Thomas really wants me to take it off the premises. (*She pulls the book towards her.*)

QUARTERMAINE. Oh. Righto. (*He begins to wander up and down, gaze out of the French windows etc.*)

MELANIE *writing, glancing occasionally at him. She is, in fact, anxious for him to be gone. There are occasional cries and sounds of* WINDSCAPE's *voice from the garden, 'Oh yes,*

yes, right to the very beginning,' to which MELANIE
responds by lifting her head, or stopping writing.

QUARTERMAINE. I say, Melanie — do you like *The Cherry
Orchard*?

MELANIE. Loathe it.

QUARTERMAINE. Oh. Why?

MELANIE. All that Russian gloom and doom and people
shooting themselves from loneliness and depression and that
sort of thing. But then mother says I don't understand
comedy. I expect she's right.

QUARTERMAINE. How is mother?

MELANIE. Oh, top hole, thanks. (*Automatically.*)

QUARTERMAINE. Well, if there's ever anything I can do —
you know — if she wants company when you want to go
out —

MELANIE. That's very thoughtful of you, St. John, thank you.

QUARTERMAINE. No, no — I'd enjoy it — I say, that is an
impressive tome old Thomas has lent you, what are you
copying out exactly?

MELANIE. Recipes. This one's for roasted swan.

QUARTERMAINE. Oh. For a dinner party?

MELANIE. No, no, St. John, it's for my British Life and
Institutions lot, to give them some idea of a Medieval
banquet. Swans are protected birds, you know, these days.

QUARTERMAINE. Oh yes, of course they are. (*He laughs.*)
Fancy thinking you'd give them for a — a — oh Lord! But
aren't they the most — most beautiful creatures. I was
looking at one — oh, just the other day, you know — on the
Cam — drifting behind a punt — and they were all shouting
and drinking champagne and — and it was just drifting
behind them — so calm — and I remember there used to be
oh! a dozen or so — they came every year to a pond near my
aunt's — when I was — was and I could hear their wings —
great wings beating — in the evenings when I was lying in bed

— it could be quite — quite frightening even after I knew
what was making the noise — and then the next morning
there they'd be — a dozen of them or so — drifting — drifting
around — and it was hard to imagine — their long necks
twining and their way of drifting — all that — that power —
those wings beating — I wonder where they went to. I'd like
to know more about them really. Where they go, what they —

MELANIE. St. John, please don't think me fearfully rude, but
I must try and finish this and I can't write and talk at the
same time, you see.

QUARTERMAINE. What? Oh — oh sorry, Melanie, no, you're
quite right, I can't either. Anyway, I ought to be getting
on —

MELANIE. Yes, with such a full evening. I do hope you enjoy it.

QUARTERMAINE. Well — well 'night Melanie, see you Monday.
And don't forget about your mother — any time —

MELANIE. I won't, St. John, goodnight.

QUARTERMAINE *goes.*

MELANIE *sits, not writing, as:*

QUARTERMAINE (*off*). I say, Henry, any chance of a game?

WINDSCAPE (*off*). Actually, I've just finished, I'm afraid —
perhaps next week.

QUARTERMAINE (*off*). Right, I'll hold you to that. 'Night.

WINDSCAPE (*off*). 'Night.

QUARTERMAINE (*off*). Oh, by the way, if you want any
baby-sitting done during the weekend, I'll try and make myself
available —

WINDSCAPE (*off*). Righto, I'll put it to Fanny — I know she's
quite keen to see the *Uncle Vanya* at the Arts — perhaps
tomorrow night —

QUARTERMAINE (*off*). *A votre disposition.* 'Night.

WINDSCAPE (*off*). 'Night.

MELANIE, *during this, has got up, gone to the French windows and during the latter part hurries back to the table, sits down, pretends to continue transcribing.*

WINDSCAPE *enters through the French windows. He stops on seeing MELANIE, braces himself, then enters properly, jovially.*

WINDSCAPE. Hello Melanie, my dear, I thought everyone had gone.

MELANIE. How are they taking to the croquet?

WINDSCAPE. At the moment they find it a bit sedate, I think, but another time or two around and they'll discover just how much — how much incivility is possible on our tranquil English lawns. (*He laughs, embarrassed.*) Now I must sort myself out — I promised Fanny I'd be home by six — now where's my briefcase — ah, yes — and a pile of unseens I seem to remember — (*Going to his locker.*) to be marked by Monday —

MELANIE. How is Fanny?

WINDSCAPE. Oh, very well, thanks, very well — a bit tired in the evenings, what with the children on the one hand and her two hours voluntary with the O.A.P's — but she's enjoying every minute of her day —

MELANIE. Good! — And the children — are all well?

WINDSCAPE. Oh yes — they're fine! Susan's a little tense at the moment, actually, with her 'O' levels — a pity she's taking them so early, I think, but she insists — she's in with a particularly bright lot and doesn't want to fall behind or let herself down so she works away until all hours. Quite often after Fanny and I have gone to bed. But she's developing quite an interest in — in — well, philosophical speculation, I suppose it is, really — the other evening — (*Bending down during this to put on his clips.*) she suddenly insisted — in the middle of supper — she'd been very quiet until then — she suddenly insisted that we couldn't prove that other people existed — and that perhaps when we thought about them or remembered them or saw and heard them even — we were actually just making them up — and of course I took her up on this and attempted to explain how it is we do know that other people exist including people we don't know exist, if you follow — (*Laughing.*) and she kept saying 'But you can't prove it, Daddy, you can't actually prove it!' And she was right. I found myself getting quite tangled in my own arguments.

MELANIE. I've always thought she was the one who takes most after you.

WINDSCAPE. Yes, yes — perhaps she does, perhaps she does — I'm afraid I rather like to think so anyway — but you haven't seen them for ages have you, you really must come over sometime soon — Fanny would love to see you again. We all would.

MELANIE. That would be lovely.

WINDSCAPE. I'll get Fanny to give you a ring over the weekend or —

MELANIE. Good.

WINDSCAPE. Right — well, oh, by the way, I've been meaning to ask — how is your mother's day-nurse working out, with the name out of Dickens?

MELANIE. Nurse Grimes. Well enough so far — she seems a very efficient, cheerful little soul — a little too cheerful for my taste perhaps, as apparently she belongs to one of those peculiar revivalist sects that seem to be springing up all over the place now — you know, meeting in each other's homes and chanting prayers and dancing about in their love of God.

WINDSCAPE. Oh Lord.

MELANIE. At least that's how she describes it — but Mother seems to like her.

WINDSCAPE. Well, that's the main thing, isn't it?

MELANIE. Yes. Yes it is.

WINDSCAPE. Well do give her my — my very best — see you Monday, Melanie, my dear.

MELANIE. See you Monday, Henry.

> WINDSCAPE, *carrying papers, books, etc., goes off left. The sound of the door closing.*

> MELANIE *sits. She lets out a sudden wail, and then in a sort of frenzy, tears at the page of the book from which she's been copying, sobbing. She checks herself as: the sound of the door opening.*

WINDSCAPE (*laughing*). What on earth can I be thinking of — going off with all these in my arms and leaving my briefcase behind — I do that sort of thing more and more now — perhaps it's premature senility — (*Entering, going to the briefcase, shovelling the papers and books in.*) or did I get switched on to the wrong track and think I was going off to teach a class — I must have as I went out that way — (*He looks at her smiling. Little pause.*) Melanie — Melanie — (*He hesitates, then goes to her, leaving the briefcase on the desk.*) Is something the matter?

MELANIE. She hates me, you see.

WINDSCAPE. Who?

MELANIE. Mother.

WINDSCAPE. Oh Melanie, I'm sure she doesn't.

MELANIE. When I get home in the evenings — do you know what she does? She sits there for hours refusing to speak — then when I get her supper on the table — she refuses to eat. I know she can only work one side of her face now, but she can eat perfectly well. And when I try to feed her — she lets the food fall out of her mouth, and — and stares at me with such malevolence, until suddenly she'll say something — something utterly — Last night she said 'It's not my fault you've spent your life in my home. I've never wanted you here, but as you're too stupid and too unattractive to make any reasonable man a wife, I accepted the responsibility for you. And now I need you at last, you refuse to pay your debt.' And coming out of the side of her mouth like a — like a gangster in one of those films you used to take me to. And she wets herself. She wets herself all the time.

WINDSCAPE. Oh Melanie, I'm so sorry. Of course I realised
that last attack must have left her more — more incapacitated
— and — possibly even a little incontinent —

MELANIE. She's not incontinent, Henry. She does it on
purpose. Out of spite. She never does it with Grimes. Only
with me. She says that as I'm behaving like a neglectful
parent, she'll behave like a neglected child. The only child
I'll ever have. Of course, she adores Grimes — or at least she
pretends to. And she's started giving her things — things
that belong to me she knows I love. The buttons from
Daddy's uniform or, the other day, a silly lithograph of a
donkey that's hung in my room all my life almost — of
course Grimes gives them back but — but — the worst thing is
I'm beginning to hate her. To hate going home or when I'm
there have such dreadful feelings. Because the thought of
years — it could be years apparently — years of this — and so
wishing she would have another attack and die now —
dreadful — too dreadful — almost imagining myself doing
something to — get her out of the way.

WINDSCAPE. She must love you really, mustn't she, or she
wouldn't — wouldn't resent your being away from her so
much —

MELANIE. But I can't give up my teaching, Henry, I can't.
Your getting me this job was the best thing that ever
happened to me. Of course she always despised it. Even
before she was ill she used to say teaching foreigners was a
job for failures — but I love it and I'm not going to give it up.

A pause.

WINDSCAPE. I only wish I could give you some comfort, my
dear.

MEALNIE. You do, Henry. Your just being here and knowing
that you — that you care about me makes all the difference.
All the difference. It always has. (*She begins to cry.*) What a
fool I was not to — not to marry you when you gave me the
chance — I keep thinking of it now — and what she said
about your being too young and not knowing what you were
doing — and blighting your career — even then she was my

enemy — my real enemy. Of course I'm happy that you're so
happy — I wouldn't have been able to make you so happy, I
know — (*Sobbing.*) I'm sorry, sorry —

WINDSCAPE (*hesitates, then with reluctance puts his arms around
her*). There there, my dear, there there — mustn't think of the
past — it's the — the future — the future — there there —

The telephone rings.

(*After a moment.*) Perhaps I'd better — perhaps I'd better —
um — (*Releasing himself, he picks up the telephone.*) Hello.
Oh Hello Nigel, yes it is! No Anita's gone I'm afraid — at
least I think she has — have you seen Anita in the last half
hour —

MELANIE, *now handkerchiefing her tears, shakes her head.*

Melanie hasn't seen her either so I'm fairly sure — yes of course
I will. (*He listens.*) You're 'phoning from Liverpool Street
and you're about to catch the 6.13 so you'll be home before
eight, right, got that — but if Melanie or I do see her by any
unlikely — yes, right, goodbye — and oh, Nigel, good luck with
your first issue. We're all looking forward to it enormously —
yes — goodbye. (*He hangs up.*) That was Nigel — for Anita — as
you probably realised and — and anyway she's certainly left,
hasn't she — Look Melanie, you must come around, and have a
real — a real talk with Fanny — take you out of yourself —
away from your problems —

MELANIE. Thank you, Henry.

WINDSCAPE. No, we'd love to see you, I'll get her to ring you.
All right? And now I must — I really must —

MELANIE. Yes, you must get back.

WINDSCAPE. Yes. See you Monday, my dear.

MELANIE. Monday, Henry.

WINDSCAPE *looks around vaguely for a moment, then goes
out through the French windows.*

MELANIE *stands for a moment, then sees the briefcase,
registers it, takes it to* WINDSCAPE's *locker, puts it in, goes*

back to the book, looks down at it, tries futiley to sort it out, pressing the page flat with her hand, as she does so.

The sound of the door opening, footsteps.

MELANIE (*closes the book quickly, gathers herself together*). Oh, hello Eddie! (*Brightly.*)

LOOMIS. Thomas is not here then — I can't make out — I've been everywhere, everywhere, up to the flat, all the class-rooms and in the office — and the 'phone going all the time about some of our Japanese and that French restaurant, and they're not even French. It turns out they're from Wiltshire — and I don't know what Thomas has said to them, I didn't even know about it — he knows I can't deal with that sort of thing — and he's booked a table for the two of us tonight at their request, forcing us to take responsibility, I don't see what it's got to do with the school if a few Japanese can't hold their drink, I don't know why he agreed — it really is too all too —

MELANIE. Now Eddie. Now. (*Going to him.*) You mustn't worry. You'll make yourself ill, and it's not worth it. Why don't you go upstairs to the flat and have a rest, I'm sure it'll all sort itself out, you know Thomas, he'll get it completely under control, he always does, in the end.

LOOMIS. Yes, yes, of course you're right, my dear, thank you, thank you. And a little rest — and I'll try and make Thomas have one, too —

MELANIE. That's right, Eddie, you both need it — oh, and would you give this back to him when you see him, and tell him I'm terribly sorry (*As she collects her briefcase and hands LOOMIS the book.*) a page of it seems to have got torn — our Mr Meadle insisted on snatching it out of my hands and then dropped it — he was only trying to be helpful of course — but you know how clumsy he is —

LOOMIS. Oh — oh dear, Cussons' — one of our favourite books, Thomas will find it difficult to forgive Meadle. Oh, by the way, how's mother?

MELANIE. Oh, top hole, thanks Eddie.

LOOMIS. Good, good.

MELANIE. See you Monday.

LOOMIS. See you Monday. (MELANIE *goes off, left.* LOOMIS *looks at Cussons' and turns to see* QUARTERMAINE *standing at the French windows.*

QUARTERMAINE. Hello Eddie.

LOOMIS. Hello St. John. I thought you'd left.

QUARTERMAINE. No — I just thought I'd see if there was anyone still about.

LOOMIS. No, they've all gone.

QUARTERMAINE. Ah.

LOOMIS. Goodnight then, St. John.

QUARTERMAINE. Goodnight, Eddie. See you Monday.

LOOMIS. See you Monday.

LOOMIS *goes off, left.* QUARTERMAINE *stands for a moment. A distant spire chimes.* QUARTERMAINE *goes to his chair, sits, crosses his legs and lies back.*

Lights.

Curtain.

ACT TWO

Scene One

The following year, towards summer. It is a Monday morning, about nine-thirty.

There have been a few improvements, different pictures perhaps; a record player, with a record rack consisting of poetry readings and Shakespeare plays. There is also a large new tape-recorder, sophisticated for the period.

QUARTERMAINE is seated, staring ahead.

WINDSCAPE enters through the French windows, carrying a briefcase, smoking a pipe, wearing bicycle clips.

WINDSCAPE. Hello St. John. (*He goes to his locker.*)

QUARTERMAINE (*doesn't respond at first, then takes in* WINDSCAPE). Oh, hello — um (*He thinks.*) Henry.

WINDSCAPE (*turns, looks at him*). Deep in thought?

QUARTERMAINE. Mmmm? Oh. No, no — just — just — you know.

WINDSCAPE. Ah. Did you have a good half term?

QUARTERMAINE. Oh. Yes thanks. Yes.

WINDSCAPE. What did you do? Did you go away? (*Going to his locker.*)

QUARTERMAINE. Well, I — I — no, I stayed here.

WINDSCAPE. Here!

QUARTERMAINE. Yes.

WINDSCAPE. Oh, in Cambridge, you mean? Just for a moment I thought you meant actually *here* — in this room — I think, perhaps because the last time I saw you, you were sitting in exactly the same place in very much that position — as if you haven't moved all week.

QUARTERMAINE. Oh. (*He laughs.*) But I say — good to be back, isn't it?

WINDSCAPE. Well, I could have done with a little longer myself.

QUARTERMAINE (*watches* WINDSCAPE *at the locker*). I say, Henry, what did you do for the half?

WINDSCAPE. Mmmm? Oh nothing very exciting really, we packed ourselves into the caravan and took ourselves off to a spot we'd heard about in Norfolk —

QUARTERMAINE. That sounds terrific!

WINDSCAPE. Yes — yes — well, the trouble was that it rained fairly steadily — all week, in fact — so we didn't get out as much as we would have liked — a shame really as among other things we were hoping that a few jaunts would cheer Susan up.

QUARTERMAINE. Oh — is she a bit low then?

WINDSCAPE. Yes yes — well she's still brooding over her 'O' level results — we keep telling her that at her age six positive passes — I mean threes and fours — is jolly good — but she seems to feel she's let herself down — but I'll tell you what we did see — it really was most — extraordinary — one morning at about six it was, I was up trying to plug the leak — it was right over little Fanny's bunk — and so she was awake and so was Ben — and Susan hadn't slept at all — so it was all rather — rather fraught, with tempers fraying — but Fanny she'd gone outside to the loo, as a matter of fact — and suddenly she called us — all of us — told us to put on our wellies and macs and come out and look — and we did — and there — silhouetted against the sky was the most — the most —

MEADLE *enters through the French windows in bicycle clips, carrying a briefcase.*

MEADLE. Greetings, Henry, St. John.

QUARTERMAINE. Hello, old chap.

WINDSCAPE. Hello, Derek. Have a good holiday?

MEADLE. Yes, thanks, Henry, very, very good indeed. What

about you? (*He goes to his locker, taking off clips, etc.*)

WINDSCAPE. Yes, I was just telling St. John, we went to
Norfolk, a little wet, but there really was one very remarkable
— well, moment is all it amounted to really. In temporal terms.

MEADLE. Sounds marvellous. Thomas isn't around yet, is he?

WINDSCAPE. He wasn't in the office when I came through, have
you seen him, St. John?

QUARTERMAINE. Mmmm?

WINDSCAPE. Thomas. Have you seen him?

QUARTERMAINE. No no — but I expect he's here somewhere.
I say — I say, Dennis, did you have a good holiday?

MEADLE. Who's Dennis, St. John? (*He laughs.*)

QUARTERMAINE. Mmmm?

WINDSCAPE. You said Dennis, instead of Derek. And he's
already said he had a very good holiday.

QUARTERMAINE. Oh. What did you do?

MEADLE. I went to Sheffield, as a matter of fact.

WINDSCAPE. Sheffield, I know it well, Fanny and I went there
the year before Susan was born, we were doing a tour of out-
of-the-way urban domestic architecture, I've got great affection
for Sheffield, what were *you* doing there?

MEADLE. Um — oh. Attending my aunt's funeral, as a matter
of fact.

QUARTERMAINE. What?

WINDSCAPE. Oh Derek, I'm so sorry. How upsetting for you.

MEADLE. Yes, it was. Very. Very.

WINDSCAPE. But when I asked you just now you did say — I
suppose it was merely social reflex — that you'd had a good
half-term —

MEADLE. Yes, well actually I met someone there I used to know.
And I managed to see quite a lot of her. That was the good
part of it. Not my aunt's death, I need hardly say. (*He laughs.*)

WINDSCAPE. Ah.

QUARTERMAINE. Who was she?

MEADLE. Oh, just a girl St. John — we were at Hull University together, as a matter of fact, she was doing the library course but we — we lost contact, for various reasons. Although I hadn't forgotten her. And when I had to take back all my poor aunt's books — there she was. Behind the counter.

QUARTERMAINE. What was she doing there?

MEADLE. Well, stamping the books in and out of course. What do you think she was doing? (*With a mitigating laugh*.)

WINDSCAPE. Oh don't worry about St. John, one of his absent days, eh St. John?

QUARTERMAINE. What Henry?

WINDSCAPE. But how nice for you to bump into her like that, especially under those circumstances, eh?

MEADLE. Yes, I can't tell you what a — a blessing it turned out to be. As soon as she was off work she'd come over and sit with me and my uncle, and on a couple of evenings when I had to go out and console some of my aunt's friends, she came and sat with him anyway, by herself. He's very keen on football, but he can't follow it in the newspapers as his eyesight's nearly gone and they're too quick for him on the radio. So she'd read out all the teams and their scores. Which was very tiring for her, as she's got a bit of a speech impediment actually.

WINDSCAPE. What a nice girl she sounds, eh, St. John?

QUARTERMAINE. What, Henry?

WINDSCAPE. What a nice girl Derek's friend sounds.

QUARTERMAINE. Oh — oh yes, smashing, smashing. Um, tell me — tell me — what — what are her legs like?

MEADLE. What!

WINDSCAPE. Good heavens, St. John, what an extraordinary question!

QUARTERMAINE. Oh yes, — oh — I'm sorry — I was just trying to imagine — I have a sort of thing about girls' legs, you see.

(*He laughs apologetically.*) I can't stand them if they're
dumpy or stumpy.

MEADLE. Well, let's just say, shall we, St. John, (*Manifestly
exercising smiling control.*) that Daphne's legs happen to
be my sort of legs.

A pause.

QUARTERMAINE. Your sort of legs. (*He looks at* MEADLE's
legs.)

MEADLE. The sort of legs I happen to like. But I don't want to
dilate on the subject of Daphne's legs (*He laughs.*) at least
just at the moment — look, St. John, I wonder if you'd
mind, there's a matter I was very much hoping to have a
conversation with Henry about. As a matter of fact, it's
rather urgent.

QUARTERMAINE. Oh. No. Sorry. Go ahead.

MEADLE. Well the thing is, St. John, it's — it's of a confidential
nature.

QUARTERMAINE. Oh — oh well, I'll go and have a little stroll
then, in the garden. (*Getting up.*) To tell you the truth my
head feels a little — a little — as if it could do with some air.

MEADLE. Thanks very much, St. John, very decent of you.

QUARTERMAINE (*going off*). Oh, not at all — but I say — I
say — (*Exiting.*) what a beautiful morning! (*He goes out.*)

MEADLE (*smiling*). You know, I can't help wondering
sometimes about old Quartermaine. I can't imagine a more
charming fellow but from the students' point of view — do
you know what one of the advanced Swedes was telling me
just before half-term —

WINDSCAPE (*interrupting*). I think it would be better really —
really much better — if we didn't find ourselves talking about
a colleague and a friend — I know that your concern is
entirely — entirely disinterested, but — but — these little
conflabs can do unintended harm. I hope you don't mind my
— er —

MEADLE. Not at all, Henry, you're quite right, one can't be too careful, needless to say I meant no — no slur on St. John —

WINDSCAPE. I know you didn't, I know you didn't. But now. You said you had something urgent —

MEADLE. Yes, well, the thing is — well look, Henry, I've been here a year now and Thomas said when I started that it wouldn't be long before I'd be made a Permanent — and yet here I am, you see, still on part-time. The only one of the staff on part-time, as it happens.

WINDSCAPE. And part-time isn't really very satisfactory for you, then?

MEADLE. Well, no, it isn't, Henry, frankly. I get paid one pound two and sixpence for every hour I teach.

WINDSCAPE. But surely, Derek, one pound two and sixpence an hour isn't such a bad rate, is it?

MEADLE. Ah yes, Henry, but you see I don't get paid during the vacations, you see. I only get paid by the hour for the hours I'm allowed to do, while the rest of the staff get paid an annual salary. So even though I'm currently doing twice as many hours again as — well, St. John for example, I in fact get slightly less than half of what St. John gets, over the year. I mean, take this half-term we've just had, Henry, a week of paid holiday for everybody else but a week of no money at all for me, it was just luck that my aunt died in it, or I might have had to miss an earning week to go to her funeral and sort out my uncle you see. — And last Christmas, well, I've kept this very quiet, Henry, but last Christmas I had to be a post-man. (*He laughs.*)

WINDSCAPE. Oh dear!

MEADLE. Yes, and let me tell you it wasn't simply the work, Henry — being up at six, and trudging through the snow and sleet we had the whole of those three weeks — it was also the sheer embarrassment. Twice during my second round I nearly bumped into some students. I only got away with it because I kept my head lowered and once Thomas himself went right past me in the car — it was a miracle he didn't see me, especially as I'd slipped on some ice and I was actually

lying on the pavement with the letters scattered everywhere
— and now the summer holiday's looming ahead — I simply
don't know how I'm going to get through that. Or at least
I do. I've already sent in my application to be an Entertain-
ments Officer at a holiday camp in Cleethorpes.

WINDSCAPE. Oh, have you?

MEADLE. Yes. And now that Daphne's back in the picture —
well you probably gathered from what I said that we're
pretty serious about each other — and I don't want to keep
her waiting around with a long engagement — there's been a
lot of tragedy in that family, Henry.

WINDSCAPE. Oh dear!

MEADLE. Yes, I won't go into it, if you don't mind. Not that
Daphne tries to conceal it. She's too straightforward for that.

WINDSCAPE. Well, she really does sound a most — a most
remarkable —

MEADLE. Yes, I consider myself a very very lucky man. So what
do you think, Henry — I know how much Eddie and Thomas
respect you — I'm going to try and nab Thomas for a few
minutes this morning — how should I go about it, with him?

WINDSCAPE. Well, Derek, I think there's no doubt that you have
a very strong case. Very strong. And as we all know, Thomas
and Eddie are very fair, always. I know they'd respond most
sympathetically — to all that you've told me about yourself
and Daphne — but you see Derek, the thing is —

The sound of the door opening, footsteps.

SACKLING (*off*). 'Morning. (*He enters somewhat jauntily, his
moustache now accompanied by a beard.*) Henry — Derek —

WINDSCAPE. Oh hello, Mark, good holiday?

MEADLE. You didn't notice if Thomas was in his office as you
went by, did you?

SACKLING. Yes, he was. Just come down. I like the chin. A
comparatively unexplored area, isn't it? How did you come by
it, not shaving, I trust.

MEADLE (*who has been getting up*). No, not shaving, don't worry — (*Attempting a chuckle.*) I'll tell you all about it later — and thanks, Henry, for your advice. It was most helpful —

WINDSCAPE. Oh, not at all, I'm glad if — if —

MEADLE *goes out during this, and as the door closes:*

WINDSCAPE. Oh — no — Derek! Oh — blast!

SACKLING. What's the matter?

WINDSCAPE. I think we had a slight misunderstanding — he's under the impression that I was advising him to go and see Thomas about being put on a more — a more permanent basis, and the truth is I was going on to explain to him that in spite of the — the strong claim he has — he should — well, in my view anyway — hold his horses for the moment — Of course — I do sometimes feel, strictly between ourselves, that it *is* hard on Meadle as the only part-time teacher — and we must be careful in the staff-room not to show any — any — well, make fun of him more than is absolutely necessary — if you see, Mark.

SACKLING. Oh, I shouldn't worry about Meadle. (*He's been at the locker during all the above.*) even St. John's observed that he's one of those people who always lands on his feet — even if he damages a toe in the process. The thing is to make sure it's his and not yours. Well, Henry, peace-maker, apostle and saint, what sort of half did you have?

WINDSCAPE. Oh, we did the usual sort of thing, took the caravan to a spot near the Broads. The weather wasn't too splendid but as I was telling — St. John, I think it was — there was one rather exceptional experience. To tell you the truth I've never seen anything quite like it. Fanny actually wrote a small sort of prose poem about it.

SACKLING. Really? I didn't know Fanny wrote!

WINDSCAPE. Oh yes, you see —

SACKLING. But on that subject — listen — I must tell you. I've finished.

WINDSCAPE. Finished?

SACKLING. My novel, old cheese.

WINDSCAPE. Oh Mark — well, congratulations, congratulations!

SACKLING. Thanks Henry. Of course, it's still only the first draft. But the point is I feel — in my guts — that it's the first draft of the final version and damned near the thing itself, actually. Because of the way it happened, you see. What I did was — I put everything I'd previously written — round about three thousand pages — into a box and lugged it into the cellar and started again. Completely from scratch. Just me, the typewriter and a carton of paper. I was actually quite — quite frightened. But it was all perfectly simple. No strain. No effort. Almost no thought. Just a steady untaxing continuous flow of creation. For a whole week. It was the nearest I've come, will probably ever come, to a mystical experience.

WINDSCAPE. I envy you. I once tried to write a novel — but as Fanny said my forte — if I have a forte — (*He laughs*.)

SACKLING. The thing is, though — the thing is — it proves to *me* that I'm a novelist. The doubts I've had since Camelia left — and worst of all, the envy! I'd read the reviews and seen the photographs of other novelists — the real ones, who'd been published — some of them people I knew, had been up with — God, there's a man at Trinity — an absolute imbecile — his *second* novel came out last month, well received too — and when I saw his face in the middle of some interview he'd given — the same imbecile face, with a smirk added — that I used to see opposite me in Hall I — I — well, I'd better not go into what I wanted to do to him. And all those women that are getting published everywhere — everyone, everyone but me, that's what I began to think — as if they'd got something, through some genetic accident — like an extra gland or double joints — that I hadn't. And so they could do it, again and again while I was working away like some — some drudge — some lunatic drudge who'd given up his wife and child and hours and hours of his life — and would go on and on drudging, through thousands and thousands of pages, not one of them publishable, to the end of my life — so I suppose that what I've discovered at last is my — well, let's use the word. My talent. Perhaps it's been growing down there, in the dark, all this time — until finally it's strong enough to take over, eh? Anyway, now all I've got to do is a bit of pruning, no doubt some tightening up — correct the spelling and the typing mistakes, and float an extract or two in Nigel's currently fashionable little magazine — I've been promising him for years — (*He laughs.*)

QUARTERMAINE *enters through the French windows.*

QUARTERMAINE. All clear, then?

WINDSCAPE. What — oh good Heavens, St. John — yes, yes, I forgot that you were still out there.

QUARTERMAINE. Oh no — I enjoyed it — to tell the truth it seems to have cleared my head.

WINDSCAPE. Oh good.

QUARTERMAINE. Hello Mark.

SACKLING. Hello St. John. Have a good holiday?

QUARTERMAINE. Yes — yes — terrific thanks. Terrific. And how were they?

SACKLING. Who?

QUARTERMAINE. Camelia. And little Tom too. Weren't you going to see them over the half term?

SACKLING. St. John, I'd be grateful if you'd stop referring to him as little Tom, and little Tom too — it makes him sound like something out of the workhouse.

QUARTERMAINE. Oh right — right.

WINDSCAPE *during this goes to his briefcase, takes out books, puts the briefcase and other books into his locker.*

SACKLING. Actually, they were unavailable. He was getting over mumps, or so at least Camelia claimed, so she took him to a friends' to convalesce. They have a cottage by the sea, and of course I couldn't offer him that, could I?

QUARTERMAINE. Um — but what a pity I didn't know you were stuck in Cambridge over the half, we could have got together.

ANITA *enters through the French windows.*

SACKLING. Hi, Anita!

QUARTERMAINE. Hello, Anita!

WINDSCAPE. Anita, my dear —

ANITA *takes off her coat.*
She is pregnant.

SACKLING. — you're swelling along pleasantly. Rapidly too.

ANITA *laughs.*

QUARTERMAINE. But you look — you look — (*Gazing at her in a sort of reverence.*) I mean (*He gestures.*) in just a week, good Lord!

ANITA. Well, it's taken a bit longer than a week, St. John.

QUARTERMAINE. No, no, but I mean —

WINDSCAPE. Just like Fanny, nothing shows for ages and then one day there it is — for the world to see —

SACKLING. And how's Nigel getting on in New York?

ANITA. Oh, he decided not to go. He suddenly became convinced — he had a dream, or something — that I'd spawn prematurely, so he stayed at home and mugged up on all the texts — Spock for practicals, and Blake and D.H. Lawrence and some Indian writer he's discovered and is going to publish, for significance — which was lovely for me as I didn't have to go to my parents, I spent most of the time in the bath reading thrillers. It was lovely.

QUARTERMAINE. Oh, I wish I'd known you were here, so was Mark, as it turned out, weren't you Mark, we could have got together — but I say, I say, it's good to be back in a way, isn't it — I mean, after a good holiday of course —

SACKLING. Tell him I'm going to give him a ring, will you — (*To* ANITA.)

The sound of the door opening, closing, during this.

— there's something I've got for him. At last.

QUARTERMAINE. You don't mean you've finished your novel?

SACKLING. Yes!

QUARTERMAINE. Oh wonderful!

ANITA. Oh Mark, really! He'll be so thrilled — he keeps refusing to 'phone you because he says it's like soliciting —

QUARTERMAINE. Hello, Derek, have you had a good half —

MEADLE *enters.*

(*Laughing.*) But of course I've seen you already, I'm sorry if I was a bit — off-colour, don't know what was the matter with me — but oh Lord, what have you done to your chin, you do get in the wars, though, don't you, old man. Was it shaving?

ANITA. Derek, are you all right?

MEADLE. Yes, yes thanks — well — (*He laughs.*) apart from finding out that I won't be joining you as a full-time member of the staff. In fact, my hours are going to be cut. By over a quarter. Which won't give me enough money to survive on. Furthermore, I may not have any hours at all next month. So I'll — I'll probably be leaving you then.

QUARTERMAINE. Leave! Oh no! That's rotten!

WINDSCAPE. I'm very sorry. I blame myself. I should have explained more fully. But you were out of the room so quickly —

SACKLING. Look, we must have a word with Thomas, with Eddie — we can't allow him just to be chucked out — Henry, perhaps you could speak to them on behalf of us all —

ANITA. Yes. Henry, you will, won't you?

WINDSCAPE. Of course I'll — I'll do my best. But whatever happens, Dennis — it's no reflection on your teaching. None at all.

MEADLE. Oh, I know that. It's Derek, by the way, Henry. (*Laughing.*) But that's life, isn't it? That's the joke. How hard

I've worked. I mean, old Quartermaine here — well, according to one of the Swedes I'm not allowed to mention because it's a fraction on the unethical side to speak ill of a colleague — well, he sometimes sits for a whole hour not speaking. Even in dictation classes or if he does condescend to speak, goes off into little stories about himself they can't make head or tail of.

There is a pause.

QUARTERMAINE. What, a Swede, did you say? What does he look like?

MEADLE. Oh, what does it matter? Everybody knows that for you one Swede is like another German, one Greek is like another Italian, you can't tell them apart and you don't know what they're called — unlike me, you see — because do you know what I do? I memorise their names before their first class, and then study their faces during it, and then when I go home I close my eyes and practise putting the two together so that by the second class I know every one of my students *personally,* and do you know what else I do, I keep a look-out not only in term-time but also in my holidays — my *unpaid* holidays — for any item that might interest them for British Life and Institutions and actually make a note of them — here — in my notebook, which I always keep especially in my pocket (*Wrestling with it with increasing violence, jerking it out of his pocket, tearing his pocket as he does so.*) along with any of the out-of-the-way idioms and interesting usages I might happen across — and do you know what *else* I do — I — but what does it matter what else I do, that's what I mean by joke or life or whatever it is, because I'm the one that's facing the push, and you're the one that's on Permanent. (*During this speech* MEADLE's *accent has become increasingly North Country.*) Not that I begrudge you — it's just that I reckon that I've earned it. Look — look, I don't mean — I don't mean — the last thing I mean is — (*He turns away, possibly in tears.*)

There is silence, into which MELANIE *enters, through the French windows.*

WINDSCAPE. Hello Melanie, my dear.

QUARTERMAINE. Hello Melanie, have a good half?

SACKLING. Melanie.

ANITA. Hello Melanie.

MELANIE goes to the table, puts down the briefcase, takes off her coat.

QUARTERMAINE. Um — um — how's your mother?

WINDSCAPE. Yes, how — how is she?

MELANIE. She's dead. She died last Tuesday.

There is silence.

WINDSCAPE. Oh Melanie — I'm so sorry — so sorry —

Murmurings from the others.

Was it another attack, my dear?

MELANIE. No, she fell down the stairs and broke her neck. We don't quite know how it happened as it was after I'd gone to bed. Nurse Grimes found her there in the morning, I still hadn't got up, the first I knew of it was Nurse Grimes calling me — and — and — that's really all there is to tell. I'd be grateful if we could dispense with condolences and that sort of thing, because what I really want most of all is to get on in the usual fashion, without any — any fuss.

The sound of the door opening. The sound of footsteps, rather odd, though.

LOOMIS. Hello everybody, hello, all rested up I trust, welcome back, welcome back — but first, is Melanie here?

MELANIE. Yes.

LOOMIS. Ah there you are, Melanie my dear (*Appearing on stage. He has a stick, his glasses are tinted, and his voice and manner are frailer.*) there are a couple of policemen in the office with Thomas, who want a word with you. They refuse to say what about, but not to worry, not to worry, because I asked whether it was illness or accident, and they assured me it wasn't so your mother's perfectly all right, my dear, which is the main thing, isn't it, it's probably some nonsense to do with your car, anyway if you'd go along to the office and flirt with them — and whatever you do, don't let Thomas lose his temper. (*He laughs.*) Mmmm?

MELANIE. Right Eddie.

MELANIE *stands for a moment, then braces herself, walks off, left as:*

LOOMIS. Really! Our Cambridge bobbies, they always have to make such a solemn meal out of the most trivial business — Anita, my dear, how blooming you look, how blooming — and how did Nigel find New York?

ANITA. Oh fine, thank you Eddie, fine —

LOOMIS. Good good good, well tell Nigel how much we're looking forward to the first Anglo-American edition, and how sorry we are we've had to cut back to just the one subscription but *semper fidelis*. Henry, what sort of half term did you have — one of your adventurous caravan treks, where to this time?

WINDSCAPE. Yes Eddie — to Norfolk.

LOOMIS. Weather all right, I trust?

WINDSCAPE. Oh yes, Eddie, yes, lovely thank you, except when it rained and — and even then we had one — one amazing moment at sunrise —

LOOMIS. Good, good, especially for Fanny, little Fanny, Ben and Susan eh — and how did Susan get on with her 'O' levels, results as expected?

WINDSCAPE. Yes, Eddie, thanks, lots of 'threes' and 'fours' — and so forth.

LOOMIS. I'm not surprised, with you and Fanny behind her, give her our congratulations do, and Mark — if that is Mark I see behind a week's further fuzzy-wuzzy, lots of tap, tap, tapping?

SACKLING. Oh, well, as a matter of fact Eddie, as I was just telling —

LOOMIS. Well keep at it, we know that one day — ah, there's our Derek, but I've already said my welcomes to him, haven't I Derek, in the corridor — I gather you found Thomas?

MEADLE. Yes thank you, Eddie, yes yes.

LOOMIS. And that you got whatever it was you were so anxious to get sorted out, sorted out, at least Thomas seemed very pleased with the fruits of your deliberations.

MEADLE. Well — well yes, thank you, Eddie, all sorted out, yes.

LOOMIS. Good, good — and St. John — yes well — gather ye round — gather ye round. (*They all do so.*) I'd like to take the opportunity of saying to you, just between ourselves, and a little behind Thomas's back, so to speak, I expect you've all noticed the very distinct drop in student enrolment these last few months. This business of the Japanese suddenly deserting us has really hit us very hard — and what with all the recent renovation expenses — anyway — Thomas is slightly more worried than perhaps he's let any of you realise. We all know how dedicated he is to the future of the school — and to the future of the staff —

QUARTERMAINE. Hear, hear!

LOOMIS. — we've long thought of you as part of a family, I think you all know that we do our best to care for you in that spirit —

QUARTERMAINE. Absolutely!

LOOMIS. — and I'm sure you're all wondering what you can do to help us through this little rough patch — and the answer is, to go on giving of your very best to your teaching, and to show what students we've got that while we may not be as grand as some schools in Cambridge, we yield to no school in the country in the thing that matters most, our devotion to their devotion to their learning of our language. That's how —

QUARTERMAINE (*amid murmurs*). Hear, hear!

LOOMIS. That's how we can best serve our school at this time of slight crisis, and as I say, this strictly *entre nous,* without reference to Thomas — thank you everybody and bless you all — the bell will ring in a minute or so I believe, so — (*He gestures.*)

And as all except QUARTERMAINE *move to lockers, etc.*

QUARTERMAINE. Eddie that was — that was terrific!

LOOMIS. St. John a word of warning, I'm afraid there have been a number of complaints about your teaching — Thomas, I regret to say, received a round robin before half-term.

QUARTERMAINE. Oh Lord, that Swede, you mean?

LOOMIS. What Swede?

During this, the sound of door opening, footsteps.

Ah — Melanie, my dear, you've cleared it up, have you, what was it all about?

MELANIE. Oh yes, Eddie. All too preposterous. Apparently a group of French girls — from my intermediary Life and Institutions got hold of the wrong end of the stick. They didn't realise my recipe for roasting swan was for a medieval banquet, and actually tried to kill one on the Cam, can you believe it! Club one to death from a punt, with the intention of taking it back to their rooms and cooking and eating it! And then when they were reported to the police, blamed me. I'm glad to say that the swan, being a swan, survived. And gave one of them a badly bruised arm. Typically French.

Towards the end of this speech, MELANIE begins to laugh. All remain still. The laugh — now almost hysterical — builds. ANITA half moves towards MELANIE.

The bell rings.

Lights.

Scene Two

A Friday evening, some months later. The French windows are open. QUARTERMAINE is asleep in an armchair, papers and books on his lap, in which he is visible to the audience, but not to anyone on stage who doesn't look specifically in it.
    QUARTERMAINE suddenly groans.
    There is a pause.

QUARTERMAINE (*in sleep*). Oh Lord! (*Pause.*) I say! (*Pause, laughs. Sleeps.*)

The sound of the door opening. Footsteps.

MELANIE *enters from left. She goes to her locker, puts her books in.*

QUARTERMAINE, *not heard, or perhaps half heard, by* MELANIE, *lets out a groan.*

MELANIE *takes out of her locker an over-night bag.*

QUARTERMAINE (*lets out another groan*). Oh, Lord!

MELANIE (*starts, turns, sees* QUARTERMAINE). St. John! (*She goes towards him.*) Are you all right?

QUARTERMAINE (*blinks at her*). Oh — oh yes thanks — um — Melanie — next class, is it?

MELANIE. Heavens no, we've finished for the day. For the week, in fact.

QUARTERMAINE (*clearly confused*). Oh, I — I didn't hear the bell.

MELANIE. It hasn't gone yet. Don't worry, Eddie's having one of his very out-of-sorts days, poor lamb, and Thomas is in the office. We're safe.

QUARTERMAINE. Oh. Oh yes — I suppose I must have let them go early — always restless on a Friday, aren't they, and then sat down and — and —

MELANIE. St. John, what are you doing tonight?

QUARTERMAINE. Oh — usual — nothing very —

MELANIE. Then I'd like to introduce you to some very special friends of mine. Would you like that?

QUARTERMAINE. Well yes — yes — thank you, Melanie.

MELANIE. I'm sure you'll enjoy it — we always end up with singing and dancing, the food's delicious and the people are — well you'll see for yourself.

QUARTERMAINE. Well, it sounds — sounds terrific!

The sound of the door, footsteps.

MELANIE. Right, you wait for me here, and I'll come and collect you when I'm ready —

QUARTERMAINE. Right oh.

MELANIE. Oh hello Derek, you too — what a bunch of skyvers we're all turning out to be, eh?

MEADLE. Yes, well, it's only a few minutes off — besides Daphne's coming down for the weekend, I don't want to miss her train —

MELANIE (*exiting*). Jolly good — give her my love —

MEADLE. Right, Melanie, right — but I had a bloody near one in the corridor I can tell you. I was sloping past the office — terrible din coming from it, sounded like a gang of Germans, all bellowing away and Thomas trying to calm them down — anyway I'd just got past the door when Eddie came round the corner.

QUARTERMAINE. Phew!

MEADLE. Yes. I began to mumble some nonsense about wanting to check up on a student — but he didn't see me — went right on past — I mean, we were like that! (*Showing.*)

QUARTERMAINE. He didn't even see you, you say? Well, I hope he's all right —

MEADLE. Oh, by the way, Daphne and I have got an invitation for you — to celebrate our engagement. Now that I've got my Permanency, we've decided to make it official.

QUARTERMAINE. Oh congratulations!

MEADLE. We're getting married on the first day of the summer vac', and I'm going to ask Thomas and Eddie to be the best man. I mean, let them decide which — I don't want to upset one by choosing the other.

QUARTERMAINE. Oh terrific! And then off on your honeymoon, eh?

MEADLE. Yes. We've settled for Cleethorpes. Not very exciting, I know, but there may be a way to pick up a little money as well as have a good holiday ourselves. Daphne's keen to start saving for a house — you know how it is, there's a very practical head on those little shoulders of hers. There's a good

chance she might even come and do a bit of teaching here
— to replace me as the part-time, you see. I've already
dropped a little hint to Thomas — I think he was worried by
her speech impediment, but I pointed out that in some
respects that could be an asset.

QUARTERMAINE. Absolutely — and she'd be — a great asset
here, wouldn't she, in the staff room, I mean — she's a
wonderful girl, Derek.

MEADLE. Yes, well, I think you'll like her even more when you
meet her. Because frankly she's — she's — (*He shakes his head.*)
And I'll tell you something — I don't know whether you've
noticed but since she came back into my life I've stopped
having all those ridiculous accidents. They were the bane of
my life, even though I was always trying to make light of
them. I suppose it's — it's something to do with needing —
well, well, the right person, eh? Love. Let's face it. Love. Oh,
I'd better get going. So see you at seven for supper. It'll be
nothing special.

QUARTERMAINE. Derek, I'm very — I'm very honoured —

MEADLE. Actually, you'd better make it 6.30, as it'll be more
on the lines of a high tea. And if you could bring along a
couple of bottles of wine —

QUARTERMAINE. My dear chap, I'll bring — I'll bring *champagne*
— and — and — oh Lord, I'd forgotten! Oh no! I've already
accepted an invitation for this evening.

MEADLE. Oh. What to?

QUARTERMAINE. Well, I can't make out, quite — I was in a bit
of a haze when Melanie asked me, but she said something
about friends and singing and dancing —

MEADLE. And you accepted?

QUARTERMAINE. Well yes.

MEADLE. But it's — it's — one of those evenings. What they sing
is hymns and the dancing up and down and around and about
and then that Nurse Grimes declares for Jesus — and then the
rest of them follow suit, and then they all stand around and
wait for you to do it.

QUARTERMAINE. Oh Lord!

MEADLE. At least, that's how it went the night she got me along. She's trying to convert you.

QUARTERMAINE. Oh Lord!

The bell rings.

MEADLE. But I told you all about it —

QUARTERMAINE. Yes, but I'd forgotten — I mean she didn't mention Jesus —

MEADLE. Well, she won't let you get out of it now. (*During this, he has been getting ready to go, putting on bicycle clips, etc.*)

SACKLING enters.

Well, I'll get you and Daphne together very soon — don't worry — (*Making to go.*) Here, Mark, guess what St. John's got himself into — one of Melanie's evening.

SACKLING (*in a hurry, with books etc.*). Christ, you haven't, have you? (*He is clean-shaven, by the way.*) You *are* a chump, St. John, you must have heard her going on about Nurse Grimes and her dark night of the soul, after her mother died. Don't you take anything in!

QUARTERMAINE. Yes, yes I did, but —

SACKLING. But you didn't know how to say no. Which, if I may say so, is both your charm and your major weakness.

QUARTERMAINE. Well, you never know — it may be — may be quite interesting — one has to — has to have a go at anything really — and I wasn't doing anything else this evening.

SACKLING (*who is now ready to go*). This evening! Yes, you bloody *are* doing something else this evening. You're going out to dinner.

QUARTERMAINE. What — where?

SACKLING. At my place — oh Christ! Don't say I forgot to invite you. Well you're invited. So there you are, saved from salvation. All you have to do is to tell Melanie that you'd forgotten —

QUARTERMAINE'S TERMS

58

QUARTERMAINE. Oh, this is terrible. You mean I'd be having dinner with you.

SACKLING. You *are* having dinner with us. It's obligatory. For one thing, I told Camelia I'd asked you — she's counting on you — we all are — even Tom, I promised him he could stay up an extra half an hour especially to see you again.

QUARTERMAINE. But what about Melanie? I promised her —

SACKLING. Oh, to Hell with Melanie! It's all a load of pathetic nonsense — and probably blasphemous, too, if one believed in God. Look, speaking as one of your best and oldest and dearest, etc., — it's *crucial* that you come. Of the greatest importance. To me. You see. O.K.? Look, I've got to dash, I'm picking Tom up from school —

The sound of the door opening, sound of footsteps.

Make sure (*To off.*) that he turns up tonight, won't you? He's got himself into one of his usual messes — see you both at eight. (*Going out as:*)

ANITA enters. She has a look of weariness about her, is subtly less well-turned out than in previous scenes.

QUARTERMAINE. Oh don't say you and Nigel are going to be there too — oh dear.

ANITA. Why can't you come?

QUARTERMAINE. Well I fell into one of those dozes again — you know how they keep coming over me suddenly — for a minute or so — and — and when I came out of it, there I was, right in the middle of this — this Melanie business.

ANITA. Poor St. John.

QUARTERMAINE. Well, I can't just turn around to her now and say — 'Sorry Melanie, something much more amusing's turned up'. She was so — well — her eyes — I can't explain — oh, if only Mark hadn't forgotten! — but then I suppose he knows I'm usually free and thought — but what do I do, Anita, what do I do?

ANITA. Oh do come if you can. It's meant to be a reconciliation dinner, and you know how they usually turn out. So you'd be a great help, as the perfect outsider.

QUARTERMAINE. Well, you know I'd do anything — anything — to make sure that old Mark and his Camelia stay together.

ANITA. Oh, it's not them that need reconciling. They already are. It's Mark and Nigel.

QUARTERMAINE. Mark and Nigel — but they're such friends, what happened?

ANITA. Oh, it was all a couple of months ago. They had the most appalling row, because Nigel turned down an extract from Mark's novel. About seven extracts, actually.

QUARTERMAINE. Oh no. Oh, poor Mark!

ANITA. Of course, Nigel made everything worse by deciding to be completely honest for once. I suppose he thought Mark, being an old friend, had it coming to him. He said that everything Mark had sent him was imitative and laboured, and anyway who really cared any more about the mysteries of sex, the wonders of childbirth, the delicacies of personal relationships — it had all been done and done and done to death, there were far bigger issues. And then of course when the magazine folded, and Nigel was going through his rough patch, with the printers threatening to sue and various other things, Mark wrote him a gloating letter — and added a P.S. about the old Amanda Southgate affair, claiming to be indignant on my account. I must say, I rather wish he'd resisted that.

QUARTERMAINE. But still — but still — he has asked Nigel to dinner —

ANITA. Oh, that was probably Camelia. She never took literature seriously. I loathe the thought of it — for one thing we haven't been able to find a baby-sitter, so we'll have to bring Ophelia in her carry-cot — she's still got six weeks cholic, after four months — so it would be nice if you came, St. John, you'd make the whole thing more bearable.

QUARTERMAINE. Oh, I'd love to — and to see Ophelia — I've only seen her the once, in hospital — what hair she had!

ANITA *laughs. In fact crying slightly.*

Oh Anita — what is it — oh, I hate to see you unhappy —
more than anyone else — (*He makes to make a move towards
her. Checks himself. Makes a move again.*) Oh Lord! (*He
stands before her, helplessly.*)

ANITA. I'm all right, St. John, honestly — it's just that — oh,
the way things go, I mean. Or don't go. Nothing seems to
come out right. All the years I adored him and he couldn't
bear me. And now he adores me and I can't bear him. You
see. (*She looks at him.*) What a — what a nice man you are.
(*She begins to cry again.*) I'm sorry — I'm tired, I expect, I'm
just tired — (*Turning away, blowing nose, wiping eyes, etc.,
as:*)

The sound of the door opening, footsteps.

QUARTERMAINE (*turning*). Oh — oh hello Henry, you've
finished late — um —

WINDSCAPE (*appearing rather heavily*). Yes, I got into a bit of
a tangle with my Intermediary British Life and Institutions,
over our parliamentary system. Usually it's perfectly clear to
me but this time it all came out rather oddly. Or it must
have done, as I had the whole lot of them dismissing it with
contempt — the three or four from the Eastern bloc, all the
ones from Fascist countries — the French were the loudest,
as always — but even the Japanese — normally such a polite,
reticent man — and I don't see quite how it happened or
what I said, but it was rather hard being lectured at on — on
political decencies — and shouted at by — by — still, I
suppose it's better they should all join up for a wrangle with
me than with each other — although to tell you the truth I
found it rather hard to keep my temper (*Sitting down.*) but
I think I managed to — with the result that I've got a — a
slight heachache. After all, I was only *explaining* our
constitution, not boasting about it. I've got my own — own
distinct reservations — no system's perfect, as I kept having
to say to Santos. His father's a Bolivian cabinet minister.

ANITA (*who has been discreetly composing herself during the
above*). It's awful when they get like that, isn't it? I always

make them explain our politics to me, and then just correct their English, whatever they say — one of the advantages of being female, I suppose — (*She attempts a little laugh.*) well, goodnight, Henry, see you Monday —

WINDSCAPE. 'Night, Anita, my dear. Best to Nigel, and little Ophelia —

ANITA. And St. John, see you later I hope. Do come if you can.

QUARTERMAINE. Yes, well — I'll — I'll — right, Anita. Right. If I can.

ANITA *goes out through the French windows.*

There is a pause. WINDSCAPE *is sitting in the chair, stroking his forehead.*

QUARTERMAINE (*is staring in a state of desperation*). I say, Henry — I say — I wonder if you could give me some advice.

WINDSCAPE. Mmmm?

QUARTERMAINE. I'm in a bit of a pickle, you see.

WINDSCAPE. Oh, St. John, is there any chance you could come over tonight?

QUARTERMAINE. What?

WINDSCAPE. I'm sorry it's such short notice, it wouldn't have been if I'd remembered. The thing is that Fanny's really very down in the dumps, very down, she really does need a — So do I, come to that. It's Susan, you see. She's taken a turn for the worse.

QUARTERMAINE. Oh, I am sorry.

WINDSCAPE. Oh, it's probably just withdrawal from all the tranquilising drugs they put her on in hospital, and then her friends will keep coming over in the evenings and talking about their plans and their blasted 'A' Levels and of course there's no possibility that Susan — at least for a few years — anyway. You see — last night — we heard her shrieking with laughter at something on television. A good sign, Fanny and I thought. The first time she's laughed since her breakdown.

So we went into the living-room and laughed with her — until
we realised that what we were laughing at was a news flash to
do with some particularly hideous atrocity in — in — (*He
gestures.*) and what followed was a bit of a nightmare,
especially for Ben and little Fanny — it ended with the
doctor having to sedate her — almost forcibly, I'm afraid —
so — so I noticed *La Regle du Jeu* was on at the Arts, one of
our favourite films, so decent and — and humane — and
then a quiet dinner afterwards at the French place — just the
two of us — if you can manage it. You're the only person
Susan will allow to baby-sit, you see. She seems to feel some
— some reassurance from you. And of course little Fanny and
Benjamin love it too, when you come.

QUARTERMAINE. I'd love to, Henry — love to — but could it
be tomorrow?

WINDSCAPE. No, Saturday's no good — we have our family
therapy session in the afternoon and we all feel so exhausted
afterwards. Demoralised, really. I've still to be persuaded that
they serve a — a useful — though of course one mustn't
prejudge —

QUARTERMAINE. Sunday, then?

WINDSCAPE. Unfortunately Fanny's mother's coming on
Sunday. Rather against our inclinations as — as she's rather
insensitive with Susan — advises her to pull her socks up — that
sort of thing — you can't manage this evening then.

QUARTERMAINE. Well — I — I — you see the problem is — Henry
the problem is —

The sound of the door opening. Footsteps.
MELANIE *appears. She has changed her dress, is wearing
high-heeled shoes, some make-up, and has taken much
trouble with her hair.*

MELANIE. Well, there we are then, St. John — sorry to have
been so long — oh, hello, Henry, I didn't know you were still
here.

WINDSCAPE. Hello Melanie (*Slightly awkward.*) Oh, I've meant
to say all day how much I like that dress.

MELANIE (*smiles*). Thank you. I'm taking St. John to one of my evenings —

WINDSCAPE. Oh. Oh I see. I'm so sorry that Fanny and I have been unable to come so far —

MELANIE. Oh, I know how difficult things are for you at the moment — as long as you both realise that any time you want to come along, I've been thinking that perhaps Susan might —

WINDSCAPE. Yes, yes, thank you, Melanie. (*Cutting her slightly.*)

MELANIE. Are you all right, you look a little fraught.

WINDSCAPE. Oh just tired, Friday eveningish, that's all.

QUARTERMAINE. And a bit of a headache — eh Henry?

MELANIE. Oh? Where?

WINDSCAPE. Well — in my head.

MELANIE. Yes, but which part?

WINDSCAPE. Well, it seems to be — just here — (*Rubbing his brow.*)

MELANIE. Ah, well then it's a tension headache, Nurse Grimes showed me a marvellous trick for dealing with that, let me have a go at it. (*She comes over to* WINDSCAPE, *behind the chair.*) Now put your head back — right back —

WINDSCAPE *does so, with perceptible lack of enthusiasm.*

MELANIE. There. Now. (*She proceeds to knead her fingers into the back of* WINDSCAPE's *neck.*)

QUARTERMAINE. So that's how they do it — looks jolly relaxing, Henry.

WINDSCAPE *endures for a few seconds, then suddenly lets out a cry, leaps up.*

WINDSCAPE. No!

There is a pause.

I'm — Melanie, I'm sorry — I — don't know quite what —

MELANIE. I expect I hurt you, pressed the wrong nerve or — I still haven't quite got the trick of it, with my clumsy —

WINDSCAPE. Well — well actually it feels a little better. (*He tries a laugh.*) Thank you.

MELANIE (*smiles*). Well, St. John, we'd better be on our way. It's quite a drive. Goodnight, Henry, and rest yourself during the weekend, won't you?

WINDSCAPE. Yes, yes — the same to you (*A slight hesitation.*) my dear. Goodnight, St. John, see you Monday.

QUARTERMAINE. See you Monday Henry and — oh, if it turns out that Saturday or Sunday — well, I'm sure I'll be free —

WINDSCAPE *smiles, nods.*

MELANIE. Off we go, St. John.

QUARTERMAINE. Right.

As they go out through the French windows there is the sound of the door opening and feet, a stick.

WINDSCAPE. Oh hello Eddie, I didn't know you were about today.

LOOMIS (*enters. He is much frailer than when last seen*). Well, there was a frightful schmozzle in the office — and Thomas asked me to come down — but was that St. John's voice I heard just now?

WINDSCAPE. Yes. His and Melanie's —

LOOMIS. Ah. Well, I would have quite liked a word with our St. John. He's caused us quite an afternoon. He appears to have missed his last class entirely. His students waited doggedly through the whole hour for him to turn up, and then went to the office and berated poor Thomas — they were mostly Germans, and you know what they're like if they think they're not getting their money's worth of syllabus.

WINDSCAPE. Oh dear.

LOOMIS. Though I doubt whether they'd get much more

sensible English from St. John present than from St. John
absent — as far as I know that Swiss Ferdinand Müller was
the only student who ever felt he got value for money from
St. John, thank goodness he's stopped sending those
postcards at last, they made Thomas quite upset — but I
wonder what it was he enjoyed so much about St. John's
classes — perhaps the lack of — of — I don't know what
we're going to do about him in the end, though, if we turned
him out where would he go, who else would have him, one
does look after one's own, I suppose, when it comes to it. I
agree with Thomas on that, after all the school's our — our
family, the only family Thomas and I have between us, so
one has a responsibility for them — but a responsibility for
the students too —

*There should be a slightly rambling quality in the delivery of
this speech.*

it's so difficult to get the balance right — so difficult —
St. John's forgetting to teach them, and now Melanie's
starting up her missionary work amongst them — Thomas is
going to have a word with her too — the Catholic countries
won't stand for it, and why should they, and now our
Meadle, taking to slipping away before the bell now he's got
his Permanency, trying to bluff his way past me in the hall
as if I couldn't see him — ha — well, at least Mark's pulling
his weight now he's got his Camelia back, I never thought for
a moment there was a writer in that lad, did you? — and
Anita — really I don't know how these modern young
couples cope — but I gather Nigel's taken to fatherhood quite
wonderfully, Thomas and I saw the three of them on the
Backs the other day, a very pretty sight it was too — so — so
— good, good, — just the problems of a flourishing school,
eh? (*He laughs.*)

WINDSCAPE. Yes. Yes indeed, Eddie.

LOOMIS. Well, I'd best get back up to bed, or Thomas will have
a fit, goodnight Henry, see you Monday, bless you, bless you.

WINDSCAPE. Yes, see you Monday Eddie.

LOOMIS (*goes off, stops*). Oh, I haven't asked for a while — how's
our Susan?

WINDSCAPE. oh, responding I think — slowly — slowly responding.

LOOMIS. Good, good. (*The sound of the door closing.*)

During this, the sound of students' voices, young, distant, in the garden. They get closer as the scene concludes.

WINDSCAPE *stands for a moment, touches his forehead.*

Students' voices, probably two girls, two boys, now laughing, calling out to each other in some sort of game.

WINDSCAPE *gets out bicycle clips, bends to put them on, as he does so looks towards the French windows. He smiles slightly, continues putting on the clips, as sounds of voices, still raised in laughter.*

Lights.

Scene Three

Eighteen months later. It is around Christmas. Not yet dark, but darkening slightly. The French windows are closed, but the curtains are opened. There is an atmosphere of chill. One table-light is on.

SACKLING, QUARTERMAINE, MELANIE, ANITA, WINDSCAPE, MEADLE *are variously sitting and standing.*

SACKLING *is smoking a pipe, has a beard.*

WINDSCAPE *is also smoking a pipe.*

ANITA *is pregnant.*

MEADLE *has a plaster neck-brace.*

QUARTERMAINE *is in a dinner-jacket.*

MELANIE *is sitting, rather hunched, nervously smoking a cigarette. It is the first time in the play that she smokes, of course. She smokes throughout the scene, lighting one after another.*

After a pause.

SACKLING. It's always at Christmas, somehow, isn't it?

WINDSCAPE. Yes.

SACKLING. Oh Henry, I'm sorry —

WINDSCAPE. No, you're right. I was thinking much the same
thing. Both my parents too, but — but of course in Susan's
case I don't think the season was — was relevant. At least to
her. The blinds were always down, you see. Because any
brightness hurt her mind. Natural brightness, that is. She
could tolerate artificial light. Until the last — last bit.

ANITA (*there is a faint touch of querulousness in her voice*).
Look, I'm sorry, but I'll have to go soon, I'm afraid. I
promised the *au pair* she could have the night off, and Nigel's
probably not coming back from London until tomorrow —

MEADLE. Yes, I've got to get back pretty soon. Daphne's
not too grand, what with her morning sickness and all the
redecorating — she's been over-doing it and I promised — I
don't want to leave her alone too long.

WINDSCAPE. Of course — of course — there's really no need for
all of us when it comes to it — it's just that — that — as soon as
I heard I had some idea that you would want — well — without
perhaps enough consideration — it was a bad idea, perhaps —

QUARTERMAINE. Oh, I say Henry — well, I'm jolly glad you
got in touch with me — though of course I wasn't doing
anything in particular —

SACKLING. Well, I must say it St. John, (*Smiling.*) you do look
as if you might have been about to be up to something —

QUARTERMAINE. What? Oh — (*He laughs.*) well, no, no, not
really — it was just — just —

During this, the sound of the door opening.

They all look towards it, as footsteps, dragging feet, a stick.

LOOMIS (*in an over-coat, with his stick, and with a deaf-aid
attached to his glasses*). I saw the lights on so I guessed
that some of you — one or two perhaps — had come. But I
didn't expect all of you. Not at this time of year, with your
families and responsibilities. Thomas would have been so
touched. So touched. My thanks on his behalf. My thanks.
(*Little pause.*) He died an hour ago. They did everything they
could, right to the end, but of course, as we've all known for
some time, there was nothing to be done. (*Little pause.*) You

know how much you all meant to him. He talked of every one of you, every evening, until — (*He gestures.*) But you'll also want to know what its future is to be, this school's that he loved so much. I know what his wishes are, we discussed them quite openly once we both knew that he was bound to leave us. I've also talked to Henry. I'm sure it will be no surprise to all of you that I asked Henry some time ago to take over the school as its sole Principal. I've no desire to take an active part in it, now that Thomas is no longer here. I loved it for his sake, you see. I'll make no secret of that. Not this evening. (*Pause, he nearly breaks down, pulls himself together.*) Not this evening. I shall be leaving the flat as soon as possible — it has too many memories — and settle somewhere by the sea. As we'd always planned to do. I hope that some of you will come and see me — (*Little pause.*) Bless you. Bless you. (*He turns. Goes. The sound of his feet dragging slowly. The sound of the door shutting.*)

There is a pause.

WINDSCAPE. I — I really don't want to speak at such a moment about plans or changes. We'll have a meeting at the beginning of term to go into those, but I should just say that I've already talked to Mark about his following me as the academic tutor. I am happy to say that he has accepted.

There are murmurs.

So until next term — which has a very reasonable enrolement, I am glad to report, let me merely assure you that I intend to do my best, as I know you will, to maintain our reputation as a flourishing school. I know — I know — Thomas and Eddie wouldn't want me to let you part without wishing you all a Happy Christmas.

Murmurs of 'Happy Christmas'.

Well, see you all next term!

They rise to go, putting on coats, etc.

QUARTERMAINE. Henry — I say, well you and Mark — that's quite a team, you know.

WINDSCAPE. Thank you, St. John.

SACKLING (*coated*). Well, night Henry — we'll speak. And
St. John — over the Christmas, eh? You must come round.
(*Gesturing with his pipe.*)

QUARTERMAINE. Oh, I'd love that — thanks Mark. See you
then. Love to Camelia and Tom and little Mark too.

ANITA. Sorry if I was a little edgy earlier Henry, (*Also coated.*)
put it down to my current condition and Yugoslav *au pairs*!
(*She laughs.*)

WINDSCAPE. You get home to your Ophelia, my dear, and
make Nigel look after you.

ANITA. Oh, I will, Henry — see you over Christmas, St. John,
I hope.

QUARTERMAINE. Oh Lord yes — lovely — lovely — 'night,
Anita and love to little Ophelia and Nigel too.

MEADLE (*coated*). Sorry Daphne couldn't make it, Henry. She
wanted to, of course. But I'll fill her in, don't worry, she's
very much looking forward to her courses next term —

WINDSCAPE. And I'm looking forward to having her join us.
Goodnight, Derek.

MEADLE. Drop around when you feel in the mood, St. John.
Lots of paint-brushes for you to wield — (*He laughs.*)

QUARTERMAINE. Terrific! I love the smell of paint — love to
Daphne —

MELANIE (*comes up, hunched, smoking*). 'Night Henry. 'Night.

WINDSCAPE. Night Melanie my dear. And perhaps we can all
get together after Christmas — Fanny was saying how much
she'd like to see you, after all this time.

MELANIE. Love to, love to, and St. John, if you're free pop
around and have a drink. (*She laughs.*)

QUARTERMAINE. Oh yes please Melanie — I'd like that.

WINDSCAPE. Well St. John where were you off to tonight by
the way?

QUARTERMAINE. Oh Lord, nowhere Henry. (*He laughs.*) You

see, there was a suitcase I still hadn't unpacked — it's been
down in Mrs Harris' cellar all these years. But suddenly she
wanted the space, so she made me take it upstairs, and of
course I opened it and there was this. (*Indicating the dinner-
jacket.*) So I decided to try it on, to see if it still fits. And
then you 'phoned, so — so I came straight over here, forgetting
I had it on. Stinks of moth-balls, I'm afraid, but not a bad
fit, eh? Might come in useful sometime. But I say, poor old
Eddie, poor old Eddie. Wasn't he — wasn't he terrific!

WINDSCAPE. Yes. Indeed. (*A slight pause.*) St. John. St. John.
I've been worrying about this for — oh, ever since I realised
I was to take over from Eddie and Thomas. If I'm to be
Principal, I have to run the school in my own way, you see.

QUARTERMAINE. Oh, I know that, Henry. We all do.

WINDSCAPE. And — and — I don't see, you see — however fond
of you I happen to be — we all happen to be — that there's
any room for you any more. You see?

A pause.

I thought it only right to tell you at the first — the very
first possible moment. So that you can — well, look around —

QUARTERMAINE. No, that's — right, thank you Henry. I — oh
Lord, I know that I haven't got much to offer — never had,
I suppose — and recently it's got even worse — it's a wonder —
a wonder people have put up with me so long, eh? (*He
attempts a laugh.*)

WINDSCAPE. If I could see any way —

QUARTERMAINE. No, no — I mean it's no good being all
right in the staff room if you're no good in the classroom, is
it? They're different things.

WINDSCAPE. I can't tell you how much I'll miss you. We all will.

QUARTERMAINE. And I — I'll miss it. All of you.

WINDSCAPE. Yes, I know. Would you like a quick drink — or —
or — come back and see Fanny.

QUARTERMAINE. Oh, no — no thank you Henry, I'll stay here

for a while — if I may — you know — and get myself used
to — and — I'll go in a minute.

WINDSCAPE (*hesitates, looks at* QUARTERMAINE). Well,
goodnight, St. John.

QUARTERMAINE. Goodnight, Henry, see you next — (*He
gestures.*)

WINDSCAPE *goes off. The sound of feet, door opening and
closing.*

Oh Lord!

Well — I say —

Oh Lord!

Lights.

Curtain.